Rolf Boldrewood

A Sydney-side Saxon

Rolf Boldrewood

A Sydney-side Saxon

ISBN/EAN: 9783337103415

Printed in Europe, USA, Canada, Australia, Japan

Cover: Foto ©Andreas Hilbeck / pixelio.de

More available books at **www.hansebooks.com**

A
SYDNEY-SIDE SAXON

BY

ROLF BOLDREWOOD

AUTHOR OF 'ROBBERY UNDER ARMS,' 'THE SQUATTER'S DREAM,'
ETC.

London

MACMILLAN AND CO.

AND NEW YORK

1891

All rights reserved

First Edition, August 1891
Reprinted September and October 1891

CONTENTS

CHAP.		PAGE
	INTRODUCTION—'BANDRA JIM,' LOQUITUR .	1
I.	JOB CLAYTHORPE, OF APPLEGATE, PLOUGHMAN	7
II.	JESSE CLAYTHORPE, CROWBOY . . .	30
III.	MR. BUFFRAY, OF BANDRA, N. S. WALES .	48
IV.	AT SEA FOR THE FIRST TIME . . .	58
V.	MR. J. ROPER, OF YUGILDAH . . .	74
VI.	MR. BURDOCK, OF WALLANBAH . . .	97
VII.	MISS POSSIE BARKER, OF BOREE . .	110
VIII.	COORAMEN AND THE WG'S . . .	125
IX.	JACK LEIGHTON, SWAGMAN . . .	144
X.	MORE OF JACK LEIGHTON . . .	169
XI.	MR. DORSETT, OF WESTBURN	188
XII.	THE FATAL LEAP . .	199

INTRODUCTION

'BANDRA JIM,' LOQUITUR

'CHRISTMAS time, and old Mr. Claythorpe, of Bandra, Willendoon, Yugildah, and a lot of other stations—for he's a well-in squatter, that took up runs or bought them cheap before free selection, and land-boards, and rabbits, and all the other bothers that turn a chap's hair gray before his time. But where was I? I'm riding ahead of my cattle. Well, the old man's having a regular count-muster of his sons and daughters, and their children and off-side relatives, that is by marriage—in fact, the whole boiling, for he always keeps the Christmas week in regular slap-up style. My word! Bandra House is big enough to hold as many again on a pinch, besides the cottage and strangers' room, and the barracks that might be stretched to carry most any number.

'It's pretty well known through the country that the old gentleman rose up by degrees like—had to work for wages when he first came to the country, like many another good man; but, instead of spending his money as soon as he got it, saved it for the start, bought a few cattle or sheep, and picked up a block of country here and there for a trifle, gradually doing better and better, through dealing a bit now and then, and using his brains as well as his four bones.

'I've heard tell that the biggest punch he ever made was by tendering for a big block of country that laid back from the frontage runs on the Logan, which the first men on the river were too dashed careless or screwy to take up. When water was got on it—dams and so on—and it was fenced, it was good to carry no end of sheep.

'Bandra Estate is where he's always lived of late years, and he bought all the land on it after he got married, and, I stick to it, THERE'S where he got the best bargain of all (the missis, not the run). No man could help doing well that married a woman like Mrs. Claythorpe; he must have had cheek enough to ask her, but women like a man all the better for that. There's no doubt he's made her a stunning good husband, and there isn't a finer family on the Sydney-side. Ten of 'em, yes, ten—six sons, every man-Jack of 'em six foot high, all married and with children of their own. They can work and ride, and take their own part, hold their own too at cricket and football, shearing and stock-riding, in a cattle yard, or outside of a horse, with any chaps in the land. And the daughters—well, I won't say much about them, it ain't my place, but we young chaps about all think a lot. Every one says they're the pick of the country side. They're all married, of course, but one, the youngest, and to my fancy the handsomest of the lot. She's tall and dark, and got eyes like a flying doe—soft like, and yet bright—but what's the use of ME pitching. I might as well wish for one of the Princesses of Wales. Hold on, though; didn't the old man tell me one day that he was as low down in the world as me when he began, more so, indeed, and that if I'd save my money, keep away from the grog, and look about for a chance now and then, I might be as well off as him some day. And suppose I DID make a rise, say in two or three years, at a diggings or anywhere, I wonder what he would say if I up and asked him for Miss Cissie. When she and I were a few years younger, and she was a slip of a girl, I broke in her first pony for her, and a regular "nut" he was, as full of mischief as a pet dingo, but she could ride him, and anything else for that matter. She had first-class hands for this start and nerve—no end. When she used to say, "Thank you, Jim, what a lot of trouble you must have taken with him, and what lovely paces he's got," I used to feel as if I could go and break my neck straight away off the worst buck-jumper on the station for such another look and a sweet smile from her. When she went away to school in Sydney, she came back regular changed somehow—more stand-off like. I dursn't look at her a'most, let alone talk. But one day the buggy horse made a bolt of it when a new-chum Englishman was driving her, and if I hadn't been pretty near, and on a horse that could go and was handy too, they'd have been smashed into matchwood. Then she looked at me so like the old way, and smiled a bit serious as she said, "You're always to be depended on, Jim, whatever happens."

'" Nothing'll ever happen to you, Miss Cissie, while I am there or thereabouts," says I, quiet and sudden like. She smiled again, and the Englishman stared and put up his eyeglass. But she took the reins and drove home, telling him she couldn't afford to have her neck broke just yet.

'Well—well, I'll have a try, I may as well run my chance like another. There's worse looking chaps than Jim Thornhill in the bush, and I might have a streak of luck at these new diggings. I'm off after the holidays, and who knows what may turn up.

'Why; what's all this? All the girls and young people have crowded round the boss, and he's going to tell 'em his history, right out from the beginning. It'll take more than one evening, or two either, still he'll get through in time. We're all welcome to come and hear it, he says, and my word he'll hide nothing, and give it 'em straight out from the shoulder.

'There he sits in his easy chair in the verandah, with the missis close by, and what a country he can look over, *every acre of it his own.* Such cattle and sheep and horses; the quality of 'em and the numbers too!

'Now he's making a start, I must close up. I'd not like to lose a word of it.'

CHAPTER I

JOB CLAYTHORPE, OF APPLEGATE, PLOUGHMAN

About the first thing I can call to mind rightly, I was living with father and mother in a bit of a cottage in the village of Applegate, near Westerham, in Kent, not far from the Sussex border, where the river Darent rises. Sister Jane was there too. There had been ten of us, but only me and she were left.

We were well scattered, sure enough. Bob, he was the eldest, had 'listed for a soldier and got killed in the Indies. Jack went to sea, and was never heard of after. Bill was smothered in a coal mine, and Joe was hurt that bad in a fight with the keepers—he being given to poaching—that he never got rightly shut of it, and died within the year. Bessie married and went to America, and Sally was in service in Rochester. Two of 'em, a boy and a girl, died young; all the better for 'em, the folks said. So Jenny and I were the only ones left with the old folks, and quite enough too, considering what there was to keep house on.

Jane was only four years older, but she was like a mother to me ever since I could mind of anything. She used to dress me—it didn't take much to do that, but she'd always wash my face and hands and keep me clean, if we were ever so stinted, besides taking me out for walks in summer, and sometimes for a great treat to Harton Wood. She teached me my prayers and Bible stories, and texts as I grew bigger. Mother wasn't strong then, she always seemed to me as if she was clean wore out and tired to death—poor mother! She was forced to lie a-bed for days and days, then she'd let Jane look after me as much as ever she liked, and a good thing it was for me, I can tell you.

Father was one of the best farm labourers in the parish in his day, folks said, but he was getting old now, and couldn't work like he used to, because of the rheumatics. A man's not *really* old at fifty—see what I can do, that am many a year past that; but then I haven't led the life father *had*. No! thank God, or I shouldn't be here with all you youngsters round me, and such runs as Bandra and Willendoon, and Yugildah mine, and be your'n when I'm dead, and all the best of it secured in freehold too. Thank God again for that; and never forget, you lads and lasses, to bless the day in your hearts when your dad left Old England for good and all.

As to the life a farm labourer lives in England, where he's told in his catechism to be thankful and contented in that state of life to which it has pleased God to call him. I was reading a book written by Mr. Henry Kingsley—I always read anything with his name to it, because I once saw him at the Anderson's Creek diggings, when I went down to Melbourne with fat cattle. He was working away there at a 'long Tom' with his trousers as yellow as a guinea, and a blue serge 'jumper' on. He's a college-read man, and a brother of the great clergyman at Eversley.

So he knows both sides. What such a

man writes is worth any one's while to read. Some people say reading's a waste of time for a man who's got his living to get. All I can say is, that if I hadn't been given to reading when I was a youngster I'd never been here. And now reach me that book there about an English labourer's life. Read you what *he* says.

Well, as I was saying, father got the rheumatism so bad one winter that he couldn't work, and could hardly crawl along with a stick. He'd worked well all his life, and been proud of his work, but he wasn't a man to save. He liked his glass of beer and his pipe of a Saturday night—and now and then when it wasn't Saturday, in the village inn, the George the Fourth. And no wonder. Poor old father! it was about the only pleasure he had in life. He never had a holiday, winter or summer, that I can remember. And if he liked a yarn with his cronies and the other farm drudges, and a seat by the fire in the cosy parlour at the George the Fourth, with a clean sanded floor, No wonder, I say again. I've never a word to say against honest work. I've worked hard myself for many a year, though I say it. But work every day of the year except Sundays, and the beasts to be fed and watered then—father was a ploughman most of his time—year in, year out, with never a change or a bit of sport, and only on wages just enough to keep body and soul together—it's more than a man can stand or ever was intended to. So the old men will drink and forget their hard lives, some of them, and the young ones rebel and run away to sea, take the Queen's shilling, or go poaching, half for the gain, and more than half for the sport and danger of the thing.

Well, spite of all his hard work, and mother's too, she wore herself out before him; and seeing that she gave herself no rest, morning, noon, and night,—never spent a penny she could help, and wouldn't have drunk a glass of beer to save her life,—father went to the wall. I was nigh ten years old then, and a cruel hard winter it was. The parish overseer said he must go to the poorhouse, as he couldn't work and had no money. It wasn't likely, at eight and ten shillings a week in his best days, with food and clothes, and fire and rent for the cottage, and *everything* to find out of that. There's no hut and rations, and wood fetched, and a cook and all that found for a labouring man in England, I can tell you all. Of course, he couldn't be allowed to starve quite. He'd got pretty low and weak, but he'd have plenty of things from the farmers that used to employ him, and the squire's lady and the clergyman's wife sent him and mother soup and things, with a glass of port wine now and then, and coals and blankets. They were kind, I won't deny that, but it couldn't go on for ever. Then, one snowy day before Christmas, the overseer told father that he and mother must be taken to the poorhouse.

I remember the day as well as yesterday. I always feel as if I could cry my heart out over it as I did then. It did seem so hard! Father had worked and slaved in that parish all his life, man and boy, from the time he was able to be crow-boy, and that was young enough. He'd never had time to go to school, so he couldn't read nor write, nor poor mother either. He had been the best mower, the best thatcher, the best ploughman in the parish, and now, when he was broken down with hard work, 'screwed' as you boys would say, there was no paddock nor pension for *him*. Nothing but to spend his last years in a place like a gaol, to linger out the dregs of life within bare walls, and be parted from the wife that he had loved and honoured all his days. It was hard and heart-breaking, but there was no help for it. Everybody seemed to think it was the only thing to be done, and as natural for a farm labourer to go to the poorhouse when his labour came to an end as for a horse to be sent to the knacker's. More than one said it was a thing to be thankful for, and that we should be grateful to Government for providing a home for father and mother in their old age. But it wasn't a home. How could it be a home when they were parted from each other, against the words of the prayer-book when they were married in the old parish church? I told the parson so, when he was talking to me that way afterwards, and it made him that angry that he wouldn't say another word, and went away in a huff, like.

However, we got partly used to it after a while, but it always made me that wild, and yet broken-hearted at the same time, when I went to see them. Father walking about with a lot of other old men, some of 'em cross-grained and others that stupid they looked like the people in the county madhouse, and others swearing and cursing with every word that came out of their mouths. I thought how different it all was when father was in good work, and used to come home and smoke his pipe in the porch beside the cottage door, with the honeysuckle twining over it, and we young ones playing, and mother bustling about getting tea ready. There was not much to eat at any time; we thought a great deal of a bit of meat on Sunday—bacon now and then. But it was homely, and we were happy in the way all folks are when their home is their own, and they can do as they like there, however poor and humble it is.

That's the reason I've always said a young fellow's better off on a forty-acre free selection in this country, though he and his wife may have to work hard and live spare, than taking good wages on a station. He's got his HOME, where he can have his pigs and his chickens, his horses and his cows, and where he can sit and read his paper of evenings and Sundays, and see his children run over the grass without interfering with any one. Lord! what would father and mother have given to have had such a place, with wood and water for nothing, and timber to build a cottage, and steady work at high prices when the cash ran short from the squatters round about! We'd have thought it like going to heaven straight off. But like poor ignorant folk, as we all were, we knew no more about Australia, or Canada, or New Zealand, than the man in the moon. If we thought of them at all, it was like the Indies or Africa—hot strange countries, where there were wild beasts and slaves and snakes, and all kinds of varmint.

We had tight work, Jane and I, to make out a living that winter. Old Aunt Betsy took us in, though she could barely keep herself. You youngsters don't know what bad weather means in this happy country. No, nor poverty, nor hunger, nor a lot of things that English labouring men and women are brought up in, as one may say. When I think of the long dark days, the snow and sleet, the bitter hard frosts, lasting a month at a time, when there was no work, and as little food, or fire, or clothes as poor little creatures like me and Jane could keep body and soul together upon, it makes me shiver again. When I look back over those dark years I wonder, so I do, how we ever lived through it all.

But Jane stuck to me like a true sister, as she was, all through the worst of the time, else I'd never have been here now. She never was one to think of herself at all. She slaved away at any kind of work she could get, late or early—house-work, needle-work, dairy-work in winter, field work and harvesting in spring and summer—anything she could earn a penny by; and she never spent nothing except in clothing for herself and books for me—for even when things were at their worst, she always made me stick to the bit of schooling she managed to get for me.

'Never mind about anything else, Jesse,' she used to say to me, 'as long as we have meat and drink, and clothes to our back. You be a good boy and learn to read and write, and do sums. They're the keys of power and riches, and men's favours, I can see, if they're used right. I don't want you to be a working drudge all your life, to be shut up and made a prisoner of when you're no more use, like poor father, and you don't want it, Jesse, do ye, my boy?'

'No, Jane! I'd like to be something better,' I used to say, 'but how am I to do it?'

'You go on with your book, and learn your geography and history,' she said, holding my hand and looking up to the stars—it was always at night we used to have these talks. 'God will show us a way. But we must help ourselves and go away from this place.'

'Go away from England? Oh! Jane, how can you think of that,' I said. I was like all boys and plenty of soft young fellows in country parts. I hated the thought of leaving the place where I was born and bred.

'How could the Queen get soldiers, and sailors, if everybody was like that? We can do as much as others; England's not the only country in the world, Jesse!'

Well, as I said before, though it was hard living and struggling for the first few years, things got better with us by degrees. Jane's steady industry and the motherly care she took of me, raised her up friends in the village. The clergyman's wife told the squire's daughter about her—what a good girl she was; how her father and mother were in the workhouse, and that she kept me and put me to school out of her small earnings. They took a fancy to her. Good principle and industry WILL make its way in the world, no matter what people say. So they used to give her needlework and clear-starching to do, and made her presents of clothes and what not. The young ladies at the Hall wanted her, after a bit, to go there as under-housemaid, which would have been looked upon as grand promotion for a girl like her, in the village. But she wouldn't take it. Aunt Betsy had been very good to us, as far as she'd been able. She'd always give us a home and house-room such as it was. She had begun to get feeble and ailing now. So Jane said she wouldn't leave her. Besides she wanted to be in the way to look after me, in school and out of school. She was afraid of my getting in with bad companions, too. I was always terrible fond of hunting and snaring and shooting when I could get a chance. She was afraid I'd get led into poaching like poor brother Joe, that was shot. So she wouldn't quit me and Aunt Betsy, though her living at the Hall would have been most like a lady's life compared to what she'd been used to. The Squire's eldest daughter, that managed the house, his lady being dead, was quite put out about it.

'Surely you are foolish in refusing so good a chance of getting on in the world,' she said.

'I'll never leave poor old Aunt Betsy, Miss Walsingham, she can't do for herself, nor the way she used to, and then there'd be Jesse all by himself.'

'Room might be found for him, to help in the garden, or the butler's pantry,' said the young lady. 'He could be provided for too. You see I am really anxious to help you.'

'I shall always be grateful, Miss,' says Jane, making a curtsey. 'But I want to keep Jesse at school another year. Then he ought to be able to hold his own in the world.'

'He is old enough to earn his living now,' said the young lady. 'I hope you do not wish him to grow up one of those half-educated troublesome lads that are the pest of a village.'

'We come of a good working stock, Miss,' says Jane, quite bold for her (she was always so meek and mild, but you couldn't turn her once she'd made up her mind). 'He and I have worked hard all our lives. We shall have to work harder yet before we come to what I hope to see. But I want him to labour to some purpose, and not to wear out his life in the service of others who forget him in the hour of his need.'

'I hope, Jane,' says the young lady very seriously, 'that you have not been reading any of those abominable radical books that are written to turn simple people's brains.'

'I have read very little, Miss,' said Jane, quite respectful. 'I haven't the time, indeed, but I want to know more than I do, and for Jesse to do the same. I can't think there's any harm in that.'

'Well, I see you are a determined little puss though you look so quiet and gentle,' said Miss Walsingham. 'I suppose you must take your own way. You shall have the work as usual, and bring the boy too, he always looks so nice and clean.'

'Oh! thank you, Miss,' said Jane, who was greatly frightened at her own boldness (she told me about it many a time afterward). 'I know you are always so good to me, you'll find me always thankful to do anything for you.'

I was getting big enough then to do a pretty fair share of field-work in the summer, and used to earn a bit of money in harvest time. I began to think we should mend our fortunes after a bit. I had got on well at school, and was proud of myself, though, Lord knows, I learned little enough. But that 'little'—you boys and girls—was the making of me, and the making of the good sheep-run we've all lived on so many a year, and the good freehold estate that's come out of it. I've heard a gentleman or two say 'a little knowledge is a dangerous thing.' I don't hold with whoever wrote that at all. It mayn't be all that's wanted, but it's a *plaguy deal better than none.* A man might as well say he wouldn't eat dry bread and drink water when he was starving, because he couldn't get roast beef. Any man or woman that can read and write, keep simple accounts, and understand a map, has got hold of the levers that move the world, and it is his own fault if he doesn't prise out a corner for himself somewhere.

Talking of reading, one of you youngsters—Charley, you're a terrible boy for books—fetch me down that first one of Sir Walter Scott's novels. Yes, that's it. Ivanhoe—I've been all through the forest that's wrote about there—it's standing still—some of it just like it was in King Richard and Robin Hood's time. We haven't got those sort of things here, but I don't know that it matters so much either. Now listen to this—as is written about a station hand named Gurth—a knock-about man he was turned into afterwards, though he was tailing the pigs when he first came into the story. Here it is—

'One part of his dress only remains, but it is too remarkable to be suppressed—it was a brass ring resembling a dog's collar, but without any opening, and soldered fast round his neck, so loose as to form no impediment to his breathing, yet so tight as to be incapable of being removed except by the use of the file. On this singular gorget was engraved, in Saxon characters, an inscription of the following purport :—" *Gurth, the son of Beowulf, is the born thrall of Cedric of Rotherwood.*" '

I recollect, as well as if it was yesterday, the day I read this, with all about Gurth and Wamba, and Fangs the dog, and the place too. Jane used to be always up and down at the Hall, and as she didn't like to leave me in the stable-yard or the garden when it was wet—and it's often wet in Kent, I can tell you, if the seasons haven't changed—so she asked Miss Walsingham if she mightn't bring me into the housekeeper's room. The young ladies used to pet me a bit, and take notice of me, and send me errands, so at last I got pretty well at home in the servants' hall and passage, and rambled about as I liked. One day I found out the old Squire's justice-room, as he called it, where he used to have up poachers and boys for stealing apples, and so on. It was close to the housekeeper's room, and no one meddled with me, so I used to go and look about there and wonder at all the things. The first day I found an old-fashioned book-case all among his fishing-rods and whips and fowling pieces. The books were mostly shabby-looking, with brown leathern backs and ragged edges; but there was lots of fine reading in 'em, and that I seemed to take naturally to, like a retriever to water, or a pointer pup to partridges. 'I had to wait there sometimes till the old Squire came back from a ride, or till sister Jane had got the things ready that I was to take to some poor woman. The young ladies made me useful that way many a time, and very good it was of them. I'd never any turn for doing mischief and spoiling things, and Jane always kept me very neat and clean, so I was allowed to do as I liked pretty much. When the old Squire came upon me with a book in my hand he used to look at me as if a stray fox-hound puppy at walk had got into the house. But he never said nothing but once.

'Is that Job Claythorpe's boy?' says he. 'Your father was the best ploughman and harvest hand on the estate. Try and grow up like him, lad, and don't idle your time over books.'

I was a bit frightened, of course, but the Squire he never said nothing to me no more, so I just went on like before, and used to read anything I came across. It was all one to me. But what took most hold upon me was this bit of a piece out of this very book, where it tells you as this poor chap Gurth had a collar round his neck, like a dog, that he couldn't take off neither, and that he was *born a slave* or thrall to his master the Saxon Squire of Rotherwood.

That got over me above a bit. I couldn't get it out of my head for months afterwards. Here was a white man, just like one of the hands on the very place, *born a slave*, and made to work whether he liked it or not. His master could flog him or jail him, starve him or kill him, I shouldn't wonder, without asking anybody's leave; in Yorkshire, too? Of course, it was a long time ago, when King Richard, the Lion-hearted, was alive. There couldn't be anything like that now. But when I began to study things a bit, it didn't seem as if there was such a mighty deal changed in the present day. Wasn't father a thrall? a slave, if you like it better, though he hadn't a collar round his neck—leastways, none that you could see.

But there was one for all that. From the time he was born he was fast turning into a helpless daily drudge, a slave in reality, though not in law, like thousands of English farm labourers. What did it matter that he wasn't called one?

He was as much tied to Applegate village, where he and his father and grandfather were born, as if he was the Squire's property, body and soul. He knew no better—poor simple father, that nobody'd ever taught to read and write—than to work day after day and year after year, as hard and regular as the horses he drove at plough. When they couldn't work any more and got old, they were sent to the knacker's yard and killed for the hounds. When HE got old and couldn't work, he was sent to the workhouse. I don't see so much difference. He never knew no better than that there's rich and poor in the world, and that the rich had all the good things and the poor the rough side of life.

But I DID know better—mostly by being able to read and write. Then I came to see how easy it was to get away from the place where one was born, and how little there was to be afraid of. There was no fear of my having a collar round MY neck—a brass one or silver either. I intended to work and get money. There was no other way; but I wanted the money to take me to countries that I'd learned about, through reading and schooling, and shouldn't never have known of but for them.

Thinking of the collar did me good other ways, too. Many a time when I was inclined to take my ease and forget that I'd made a vow to work and save and scrape every penny together till Jane and I were able to go away, I'd think of Gurth and his collar, and that idleness and drinking and bad company was able to put a collar round a man's neck, and rivet it there, too, as well as ever a smith in the land. So I kept up a good heart. I made myself merry with thinking of the day I might be more like Gurth's master than the poor swineherd himself. There was no emigrant ship in his day, and no new country—only chains and flogging for those that ran away. How everything has changed, to be sure! Changed for the worse, I've heard gentlefolks say—from the good old times when the rich were kind and the poor humble and thankful. Now they were independent, ungrateful, and ready to turn everything upside down.

I'd read about countries where they'd done that too; and I didn't wonder at it, if all tales were true. I hadn't any feeling of that sort myself. I'd no edge against rich people or those above me; but what I wanted was to move to some country where I could get a chance, and have my share of the good things that were going in the world—a share of the land that was made for rich and poor alike—a share of the good houses, the fine horses, the live stock, the grass meadows, the orchards and vineyards, that lucky people owned, but that chaps like me was only allowed *to look at*, like the crossing-sweeper at the buns in a pastry-cook's window. When I wondered at fine things in England, I always felt that I had no more chance of having any of them for myself, as the wages of honest labour, than I had of getting a handful of the Queen's jewels. They were not for me, or the likes of me, and that was all about it. We might look at the trees in all their summer leafing; we might peep over the park wall; we might strap and clean the blood horses (and woe betide us boys if we left even a speck of dust on 'em); we might see the sheep and cattle and fat oxen at the big shows; we might watch the hunters jump, and the traps and drags roll round; but what claim had WE, if we lived a hundred years, and saved our money all the time, of having any of these things for our own? No more show than there was of having last year's comet handed over to us to look over and measure.

Now, and isn't it strange, I'VE GOT ALL THESE THINGS! Of course, I'm old and shaky, and can't value 'em as I ought. You get 'em when you don't want 'em, as Mr. Merlin says. But I've got the land and the big trees and the flower garden and the blood horses and the short-horn cattle and the fine-woolled sheep and silver prize cups and medals by the dozen; and how did I get 'em all? Why, by coming to Australia.

CHAPTER II

JESSE CLAYTHORPE, CROWBOY

OF course, we'd go and see the old people regular, Jane and I. Father used to keep much the same—he'd got not to bother himself much about anything but his vittles and an ounce of tobacco now and then. He'd left the world for good and all. There was no more to do in it for *him*. He was a sort of monk now without the things that monks have to keep themselves alive with. He used to ask us about the crops and the weather, and who was dead and married or buried, but didn't trouble himself much one way or the other. He had a kind of half notion that somehow or other his fifty odd years of hard work and good character oughtn't to have ended this way; but he couldn't account for it. His mind was that hazy and confused like he couldn't cipher it out nohow. He puzzled over it while he was smoking when I brought him some fresh tobacco.

'Jesse, lad,' he would say, 'I cannot unravel the weft o' it. I've made and helped make a sight of victual in my day, and now there's nought for me but a handful of oatmeal night and morning, with a bit of meat and soup like kennel stuff. Parson says there must be rich and poor all our days on earth. You and me's meant to be poor, and the Squire to be rich all along, seems like it.'

'I don't believe that,' I hollered out one day, 'and Jane says she don't neither. Anyhow, we're a going beyond the seas one of these days. WE'RE not going to stay here for ever.'

'Take thee care, boy,' said father; 'them places beyond seas is wild, they tell me. I doubt Old England's safest biding yet, though I can't say as how I've found it any too good.'

'We're going to try New England, then,' I said. 'There's too many of us here;

that's why the bread and beef won't go round. We're going to find out a new country where the land's cheap and men and women dear. That'll suit us better than this old one.'

'I doubt thou'st rash,' said father, shakin' his head; 'but thou was always a stubborn whelp, and I canna blame thee for going to seek thy fortune. Happen, thou'lt make a better outcome than I've done. If it werena for the rheumatiz that's racking the old bones of me, I'd go with thee. I'm tired of this dog's kennel life, and would as lief hang myself as not if it wasna for thy mother, and to grieve thee and Jane.'

You may be sure we saw poor mother regular. Jane went every Sunday of her life, and any other time that she could spare. Besides that, we fetched her what little things we could get—tea and the like of that. It was the only treat as she'd ever allowed herself when she was at home. She didn't care for anything else much now. She grudged our buying it out of our bit of money, but when she saw how it pleased

Jane and me, she left off chiding us for it.

'The Lord left me you two good children in my old age,' she said. 'I should have been dead if it had not been for you. A hard life I've had, God knows, but I'm not quite forsaken. May He see fit to prosper you both some day, when father and I am dead and gone.'

We used to try and liven her up, telling her of all the things we saw and heard in our small way. Sometimes she would smile and look as she used to do in old times, and then again, when she thought we'd have to leave, and the gates be locked on her, she'd cry and bemoan herself till it nearly broke our hearts. But she tried mostly to bear up, and always told us to be good children and read our Bibles, and we might be sure we should be helped and taken care of.

I don't know how she *could* think so, seeing that nothing of the kind had happened to her and father; and if ever a woman deserved it SHE did. But it comforted her to believe what she had been taught, and to teach us the same. She thought it *might* come right for us, I suppose.

Still and all, we could see that she was getting weaker and weaker day by day. She could hardly walk up and down at last, and when she rested it seemed such a trouble getting up again—and so-and-so. (Here the bluff, hearty, old man stopped, and turned his head away. It was a minute or two before he could go on.) When the winter came again—how we feared it—she had to take to her bed, and one day, a dark, bitter winter day it was, just after Christmas, we followed poor mother to the village churchyard. It wasn't much of a funeral, poor thing, but it was a better one than most of the poor creatures had that died there. Some of the village people that knew her in her good days made shift to follow her, and did their best to comfort us and father. But it was a sad sight for all that—the snow all over everything, as if the earth was dead and ready to be buried too—the shabby hearse and only the undertaker's man to drive it, who was in a hurry to get home. When the curate came to the part, 'our beloved sister,' I thought to myself, 'No one took much care of her in this world; I hope she'll have better treatment in the next.' But I kept them thoughts to myself, for Jane wouldn't hear anything of the sort, and scolded me if I said a word. 'We must be patient and do our duty and trust in God's providence,' she always said. 'We had no right to judge what was best for us. God knew all things, and we must have faith in Him.' She was right, as it turned out. She always was. But a little thing would have started me on the wrong road then of careless ways and unbelief—a road, boys, that always leads to ruin.

I was doing a bit of garden work—cleaning up the orchard for a farmer towards the end of September next year—didn't get much wages either, you be sure. Farmers never give a penny more than they can help in England for labour. They've some reason, too, for rents are high, or used to be in my time. I hear they're lower since, and well they may be, for what with Australian wheat and mutton coming in, and beef from America, not to mention cheese and butter, farm profits have gone down so, that the squires have had to lower the rents or take the land themselves. However, that wasn't so in my time.

Well, as I was saying, I heard the farmer say to his wife, 'Who do you think's come down for the season's hunting?—why, Ned Buffray.'

'And who's Ned Buffray?'

Says the farmer, 'If you fetch me in a mug of cider, while I sit down for a spell, I'll tell you it all easy and comfortable.'

She brought him the cider, and they sat down in the porch, and as I was doing some little thing close handy, I couldn't help hearing what they said.

'Don't you never remember to have heard tell of Mr. Buffray, of Barndown Farm on Stone Meadows? It's nigh half a hundred years ago, but I heard my father tell many a time of how old Stephen Buffray, after he couldn't pay the rent on his farm no longer, packed up his things, and took all his family with him to Australia. Cheddars got the farm then, and they've had it ever since.'

'Oh yes, now I do seem to remember.

Aunt Tilly used to tell us how they was such a big family, twelve or thirteen, and how Mrs. Buffray didn't want to go, but old Stephen, he was always that masterful and impatient that no one dared cross him. He said the country where a man that worked hard and never wasted a penny couldn't pay his rent and had to be turned out of his farm, where his father and his grandfather had lived all their lives, was no country for him, and it was time to try another, as his ancestor did, as he always swore was a soldier with Billy the Norman hundreds of years agone.'

'I see you've got it all quite pat. That old aunt of yours, I might ha' known, would be sure to have it and all the other stories of the neighbourhood at her fingers' ends.'

'Don't you say a word against Aunt Tilly,' says she. 'A better woman never stepped, and listening to her kept us girls from reading those silly books that all the young people spoil themselves over nowadays.'

'Mayhap, mayhap,' says the farmer, 'but I must get on with my story, or I shall never get back to the Fifteen Acre in time to see what the men's done. Well, this is a son, the youngest but one, of old Stephen.'

'You don't say so?' says his wife. 'And what's he like, and what's he come here for?'

'He's come down here for the hunting; brought six horses, a groom, and a boy. He looks to have plenty of money—a free-spoken, off-handed chap, they tell me—favours his mother's side, being square built and middle framed. Not long and lean, like old Steve, with his hawk face and fierce eyes, that used to frighten all the folks when he was in a rage, I've heard tell.'

'And how does he ride?' asked Mrs. Hedges.

'Rides like the devil; the day I saw him out cub-hunting, never saw a man go straighter to hounds. Capital hands and seat. Looks as if he'd been born atop of a horse.'

'And what's he a doin' of here? Going to buy a farm?'

'Wants to see the country, I reckon, like any other gentleman of fortune; besides, he's been to the old farm, they tell me, and Westerham churchyard, where his great grandfather, old Francis Buffray, lies buried, and has a carved tombstone with a coat-of-arms on it.'

'How did he make all his money? It's easy picked up in them parts, I expect.'

'Nobody asked him how he made his money that I know of. 'Taint our business, anyhow. He looks like a chap that's been middlin' well off all his time. Not but what he could work on a pinch if he was wanted, I daresay.'

'Well, I never!' said Mrs. Hedges. 'Who'd a thought of old Steve Buffray's son turning up here again like that? We all thought they were lost or eaten by blacks or summat.'

You may depend on it I thought a deal of this bit of talk, after all the years I had been studying where I should go to begin the world away from Applegate. I didn't want to end it there, you may be sure; and here was a whole bookful of knowledge. I had seen the tombstones of ever so many of the Buffrays in the old grass-grown churchyard at Westerham; heard, too, that the whole family had gone away to foreign parts somewhere about fifty years since; couldn't say whether it was 'Horsetralyer,' as most of them called it, or not. All they knew was that it was a long way off. Whether it was in Africa, America, or the Indies, none of them cared to know.

Well, by poor Jane's help and teaching, I had been saved from this state of ignorance. I was sharp about geography, so I looked out Australia, and found that there were divisions or colonies with large cities and houses, just like other places.

I made up my mind, once for all, to see this wonderful Mr. Buffray as all the village was in a state of curiosity about.

So I managed somehow to knock up an acquaintance with the boy who helped to look after the horses. A pennorth or two of lollies, and a lot of gossip about the stable, and I soon heard all he had to say, which was not much.

Mr. Buffray was a 'very nice gentleman,' as he put it. 'Pretty free with his half-crowns, but would have his work done, very partickler about his hosses, and knew in a minute if you'd not been usin' elber-grease up to the mark. He believes he came from South Australia, or them parts over the sea. Didn't see any difference in him, except in his ridin', which he always went like as if he'd got a spare neck in his pocket. There wasn't a man in the hunt that could get away from him once he had a start. He'd be like to get a baddish fall some day, he was so bold and careless like.'

This only set me more and more on the task of finding all out about Mr. Buffray. Here was what I wanted to know. If a large family could go to the far country after having lost all their money in England, and in forty or fifty years be so well off that one of the sons should come back to the old place able to hold his own with the gentlefolk about, why, what a wonderful country it must be, and why couldn't I, Jesse Claythorpe, go and do the same.

The next thing to do was to get Mr. Buffray to tell me something about this wonderful place. I knew it was more that ten thousand miles off. It couldn't be so foreign and strange like, because I had heard one of the gentlemen at the hunt, one day, when I went to see them throw off, say you couldn't tell Mr. Buffray from any other Englishman, except by his being a good deal tanned with the sun, and that might happen to any born Englishman that had been away from home. He looked like one and spoke like one. He wasn't above five foot eight in height, and he weighed over thirteen stone. So what was there in going out to Australia that so many folk and all the old women made such a bother about? This man knew most things about fox-hunting, and rode to hounds as if he'd done it all his life. He was mighty severe about his top-boots and leathers; depend upon it they were pretty English in all their ways where he came from.

I went over with this to Jane. I always told her everything then, and for many a year after. She knew all about Mr. Stephen Buffray's story, and we went next Sunday and saw the gravestone of Francis Buffray in Westerham churchyard. She told me of the young ladies of the Hall, who seemed to take a deal of notice of it, and showed her a book of the old records of the county, and there it was set down that the old name of these Buffrays was Beaufray, or Beaufrere, which means something about brother in French. She got some one to point him out one day as he sat on his horse Bondi, a great, fine, Irish hunter, the best of his string, and that could jump anything. And she said it was a pleasant sight to see an Englishman of a good, old stock come back to the place where his ancestors had lived and died, and show himself as good a John Bull as any of them, though he had been born and reared on the other side of the world.

'I begin to think you're a clever girl after all, Jane,' she said. 'Steady workers like you and Jesse, with a spice of ambition, have a better chance in a new country than we can give you, but be prudent and careful.'

Jane said there was no likelihood of her being anything else, and that I only wanted to have the chance of getting on in the world. She only hoped I might get a word with Mr. Buffray some day.

Miss Walsingham said she would ask her brother, who spoke to him in the hunting field sometimes, to mention my name.

Anyway it didn't come off. English gentlemen are not fond of talking about anything but the business in hand out hunting, especially to people they don't know all about. And though Mr. Walsingham knew him well enough to pass a remark to now and then about the line the fox was heading, or that the take-off at the brook was sound near the pollard willow, yet he didn't feel like going into the emigration question with him.

But I waited. The season was all before us, and till it was over Mr. Buffray was safe. My turn would come. And one day, sure enough, towards the end of the season it did come. The Mid-Kent hounds were not altogether a crack out-and-out pack like those in the flying counties, as they call them, or the shires, yet the fencing was none so foolish. There were a many double ditches where the banks were rotten in places. Then you couldn't always tell which side of the hedge the ditch was. It wanted a horse that could poke and creep, and kept a bright lookout for all the traps and drains and drops that a free-goer might break his back over.

And one day Mr. Buffray did; that's to say he had an awful fall. He looked like a dead man when I lifted up the head of him. 'Jesse,' says he, afterwards, 'if I'd died then I should never ha' known what dyin' was like.'

It was a mighty long time before the breath came back to him, I can tell you, and many a month before he could mount a horse again.

The way it happened was this. He always used to ride very fast at his jumps and take everything just as it came. This day he had taken two or three flights of rails, one after the other, when his hounds crossed a field with a thorn hedge and a big ditch. He rode at a weak place in the hedge, thinking to bore through. It was a regular bullfinch, one of those hedges a man puts his arm in front of his eyes and rides at as hard as he can like. Of course he'd have got through all right, but what had the farmer done but had what they call a 'cow hurdle' put there—you never see one in this country. A great, heavy, awkward thing stuck in about five feet high, made of strong round oak waste, tough enough too. Well, the old horse never looked for this, never saw it of course, and, hitting it hard, carried it out into the field. There he got his legs into it, and, going the pace he was, couldn't stop himself, and came a terrible cropper, head over heels, and rolled right over Mr. Buffray. Then they both lay as if they were dead. I happened to be close by, as luck would have it, and ran up. I got the horse off him, which staggered and rolled about half stunned. Mr. Buffray lay still as if he was dead, and I had to fetch water in my hat and dash it over him for some time before he looked up and could speak.

'A deuce of a cropper,' he said, trying to get up, and falling back again. 'What's your name, boy?' 'Jesse.' 'Well then, Jesse, you ride my horse Bondi up to that farm-house and ask them to send a cart down for me. I don't know what bones are broken or what ain't. Then you take him over to the Barley Mow, where I put up. Now, don't ride him fast, mind that, and leave word with the doctor that I'm badly smashed, and am at Farmer—what's his name?'

'Hopsley, sir,' says I.

'Well, I'm at Farmer Hopsley's and he's to come and see me and mend me up again. Now then, don't forget, don't ride him too fast, and come back to-night, however late it is. I shan't be asleep, I'll be bound.'

I rode away as pleased as Punch on the big bay horse. I could ride pretty well, and was handy with horses. I'd had plenty of practice at odd times, as I hoped to get taken on as helper in one of the hunting stables.

Anyhow, I did what I was told, and the doctor was out in quick time. He said that Mr. Buffray had broken his collar-bone and two ribs, besides giving himself a pretty good shaking all over. Mr. Buffray took a fancy to me from that day, and on that day my good fortune set in.

CHAPTER III

MR. BUFFRAY, OF BANDRA, N. S. WALES

In a day or two—most as soon as Mr. Buffray could sit up in bed, he sent for me to come and see him. He was pretty white and all bandaged up, but his eyes, which were rather small and gray, were bright enough. 'He was all right,' and on the mend.

'Well, Jesse,' he says, 'you did me a good turn in picking me out of the mud and holding up my head that day. I might have been smothered else, with the old horse atop of me. And now I'm going to see if I can help you a bit—one good turn deserves another, they say. Would you like to come into my stable as helper. I see you can ride, and have better hands than most young brats of your age.'

I told him 'there was nothing I should like so well.'

'All right,' he says. 'I'll give you a note to my groom. You'll have to toe the mark, or else ash plant's the word, and well laid on too. You English lads get more licking than our boys do, and you're none the worse of it. Give your master a week's notice and come to me at the end of it. You'll have to ride the horses their walking exercise, clean bits and stirrup irons, and do all you're told to do. As to wages, I'm a little above the market I know; you'll have to work all the harder.'

I went away as happy as a king, you bet. The very thing of all others that I had been longing for had happened to me. It was a lucky chance that the cow-hurdle was there, and as Mr. Buffray was getting better, no harm was done. I told the farmer I was going to a new place in a week. He said I was right to give him notice, but I could go next day if I liked. Boys were cheap and plenty in those parts, and it was more for the sake of giving me something to do that he hired me at all. So I tied up my things in a handkerchief next day, and went over to tell Jane, who kissed me over and over again, with tears in her eyes, and said she was sure I was in the right way at last. In the afternoon I went over to where Mr. Buffray's horses stood at livery, and took my share of the work of bedding them down for the night. The boy that was there was a friend of mine, and I thought I would take part of his work and so make it easier, and the groom said I had brought in Bondi cool and comfortable, and showed more sense than boys did mostly, that rode full tilt for the doctor, which was all right—and then rode just as fast back, which was all wrong. So I had a fair start.

I was determined to do my best, and not to lose a good place for want of carefulness. So I worked and slaved, night and day, late and early. I picked up all I could from the groom, who was a very smart one and master of his work; learned how to ride a second horse, and set to at a tired hunter, with many other points of stable management. Master was soon in the saddle again, and rode as straight as ever—there was a deal of the bulldog about him; and as he found I was doing my best, and getting smartened up a bit, he took notice of me, and spoke to me at odd times about all sorts of things, but chiefly about Australia, because I generally managed to edge the talk that way.

'Yes!' he said, one day as we rode home when we had had a famous run, for I had come up just at the nick of time with his second horse, and he had been in the first flight all through. 'England's the best country in the world when a man has made his money, but there's no place like Australia for making it. It's the place for a young fellow to go to that has all the world before him.'

'Are you ever going back there, sir? I said all of a sudden.

'Going back?' he says, quite quick and sharp. 'Of course I am. I couldn't live here for more than a year at a time. I didn't intend to leave just yet, but I've had letters, and I shall be off as soon as the season's over.'

'Are you going to take any horses out with you?' says I, rather fishing.

'Well, yes! None of these, but I shall take a couple or more. What do you say to coming out to take care of them? I suppose you wouldn't like to leave England for anything, like all you country boys?'

'I have been thinking of it for years,' I said. 'The only thing is, that I don't like parting with my sister Jane. If she comes, I say yes in a moment. But I must see her first.

'What's she like—anything like you?' he said.

'She's the best girl in the world,' I said, quite hot like, 'and the best sister that ever was. If she could only go, but I don't see how it's to be managed. So we'd better not think of it.'

'Do they grow much corn out there, sir?' I went on, as he said nothing, but kept studying.

'Corn? So much wheat that they send it home here to sell every year,' says he. 'Maize—also what we call Indian corn, oats, barley, and hay, any quantity; only we make our hay of green oats, not grass as you do here, and wonderful good hay it is—stronger and more fattening than this meadow grass of yours.'

'How is that, sir?'

'Why, it stands to reason,' he says. 'There's the straw and the oats both. A horse will do hard work on it with never a mouthful of corn or beans, and they won't do that here, will they?'

'I suppose they must use a lot of it for the winter,' says I, 'to feed all the cattle and sheep on.'

He laughed then. 'It's a wonderful thing,' says he, 'that all you lads grow up as ignorant of the England beyond the seas, —and it's as much England as this county or Yorkshire,—one would think it was Africa or the West Indies. Why, all the tens and hundreds of thousands of sheep and cattle never get a straw to eat in winter (unless it's a drought) but what they can pick up.'

'Then how do they live?' I says, greatly wondering.

'Live on the grass. What else? All the country's covered with grass, and where the trees grow thin it makes very little difference. They don't shade all the ground as they do here, and you never saw better beef or mutton in your life.'

'I couldn't have believed it, sir.'

'No! I suppose not,' says he. 'Because you people won't go and see for yourselves—only a man like my old father, now and then, that never trusted anybody's opinion but his own; and so you stay cooped up in this little island, with the rich getting richer, and the poor poorer, every year, and won't go to a country where there's land for nothing, and work is well paid, and every man rises in life who has hands to work, and sense enough to keep away from the brandy bottle.'

'That's enough for me,' says I. 'I'm away as soon as I can find the way, and Jane, she goes when I go. But how are we to find the money? It's ten thousand miles off. I saw that in a book.'

'Every month, sometimes oftener, there's emigrant ships,' says he, 'when the passage money is very low; there's no trouble about getting out. Where's your sister? If I saw her I might arrange to get her a place when she got out.'

I thanked him, and said I would bring her to see him.

So I went and got Jane to come with me one day, and talk over the notion of emigrating. Jane was dressed very neat, and since she had been up at the Hall she had picked up a way of carrying herself, and behaving, as she hadn't before she went. A real fresh, rosy, Kentish face had Jane, and Mr. Buffray liked the look of her face from the start. She talked so sensible like, too, asked what he thought it would cost for us to go out in the ship, and whether we'd be sure to get places directly we got out, for she didn't like the notion of wandering about in a strange land.

'There'll be a dozen places for a girl like you, and fine wages, 12s. to 15s. a week, the first day you go into the Immigration Hiring-room in Sydney. But for fear of any mistake, I'LL hire you and your brother and have a friend to meet you. Mrs. Buffray is always wanting a girl like you for housemaid, and half her time can't get one, so you're suited, and Jesse here can have charge of one of the horses that I'm taking out with me.' So we settled it there and then.

'But I can't leave Jane, not till she's fairly

out in Australia, and settled,' I said. 'I wouldn't let her go out by herself for any money. You can easy get a man for what you want on the voyage.'

'Not so easy, youngster,' says he, looking a bit put out. 'But I suppose I must let you have your own way, though my opinion is that your sister can take care of herself anywhere.'

And so she could. But I was not going to send her out all alone, whatever happened. So the end of it was, we saved all the money we could out of our wages, and by the time the hunting season was over, and Mr. Buffray was thinking of going away, we managed to get enough. The clergyman and all the gentlefolk of the parish gave us a good character, and made up a few presents for us, and we went away to the ship by the South-Eastern railway, and said good-bye to Old England for good and all.

Mr. Buffray behaved very liberally in the matter of wages. He gave me something over and above, too, besides writing a letter which I was to take with me and deliver to his agent in Sydney. He also wrote word to have us met at the depôt, and to be put in the way of going up the country to where his place was. We would have no trouble after that, he said, and he would be out himself before many months.

CHAPTER IV

AT SEA FOR THE FIRST TIME

ONCE we were fair on board ship it wasn't so bad. All the journey to Liverpool passed like a dream, and the crowd of people, the sailors, the ships, and the bustle of boats, and friends, and idlers, at starting, was enough to put quiet people like us, that had never seen the sea before, off our heads. But Jane said 'plenty of other people have had to do the same. We must keep a stout heart, and trust in God. I suppose we're made of the same flesh and blood. All we have to do is to wait and look about us quietly; we shall soon find out more about things.'

She was right. Generally she was, I found. After the first few rough jumbled-up days everything went smooth enough. Then we saw what a wonderfully made, well-managed piece of machinery a good vessel is. We made friends with some of the officers and crew. There was nothing to do, but Jane—she'd brought a small box of books—insisted upon my doing the same as she did, which was to keep up our schooling, and read, and practise a bit like, every day.

'Depend upon it, Jesse,' she said, 'it will be a long time before we have another three months like this, with nothing to do, plenty to eat and drink, and everything provided for us.'

I'd got a way of always doing what she told me, so I kept level with her, and we got through a deal of reading and such like. Some of the young 'uns asked me if we were going to keep school when we got out to Sydney.

I said perhaps we might. There was no knowing what emigrants have to take to.

We practised ourselves with geography as much as anything. I was always fond of maps, after a fashion, and once got a prize for drawing them neatly. So I kept the ship's course marked upon a chart every day, and copied out the boundaries of the different colonies. After a while I knew the ins and outs of them by heart. We read through a lot of the little books which are written for emigrants, and found a deal of useful knowledge in them—I mean, that came in useful afterwards.

Jane was that steady and solid in all her ways that she began to be taken notice of as a well-conducted, good young woman on board. One day she was asked by the doctor if she would help the matron and be her assistant, as some of the girls and younger women gave them a good deal of trouble. Jane agreed, more in the hope of doing good than anything else, and was quite surprised at being told that she would get five pounds for her services as soon as she landed. We thought it quite a large sum, and Jane expected to do wonders with it.

We had a good passage luckily, and next to no illness or disease on board. Everything went well, and as we had both been working pretty hard and regular all our lives, we enjoyed the rest and the feeling of having nothing to do when we woke in the morning

—more than we could say in poor old Applegate.

Of course we hadn't things all made a'purpose for us. Some of the men were fools enough to gamble, especially the young ones, and so lose money that they couldn't well spare.

Amongst the girls and women some were fond of gossip, and listened to foolish stories from the sailors about Australia—things which we were quite sure were not true. Out there they believed there was no differences of rank—that they would be quite on a level with their masters and mistresses, and with everybody else. That there would be such a rush to bid for their services that good servants might ask any wages—two or three pounds a week if they liked. Also, that all the good-looking ones could be married to rich squatters directly they landed. That the work was light, and often as not half-done, with a lot of other rubbish which made the inexperienced girls fancy they were going out to be treated like ladies, and that household service was done away with in the new country.

Jane and I agreed that all this seemed very unlikely. Mr. Buffray was very simple and straightforward in his ways, and would speak to anybody, but there was a something about him that prevented people from being too familiar, and none of his servants or the village people had any encouragement to put themselves on an equality with him any more than with any other strange gentleman that came there to hunt, though everybody knew he was old Stephen Buffray's son.

I asked him once whether people worked as hard in Australia as they do in England.

He considered for a bit, and then said, ' I should say that they worked HARDER, for this reason, they're paid higher wages and better fed. Masters try to do with as few working men as possible, and expect them to keep up good pace all the time. Here they're badly paid, badly kept, often not up to a hard day's work at the long hours they keep, on which account there's a good deal of what we call in the colonies " Government stroke." The farmers and gentry here are obliged to put up with it, as they don't send the labourers out of the parish. With us, if a man's not up to the mark, he's "sacked." There's no parish settlement, and nobody knows or cares where he goes.'

'And the women?'

'Well, there's no field-work. But in the house one servant does the work of two—sometimes, indeed, more. I think the Australian girls—when they're good, mind you—are quicker, smarter servants than yours, and put more heart into their work.'

'And there are masters and servants, and gentlemen and ladies, and rich people and poor people, just as there are in England?' I asked.

'Very nearly the same. The only difference is that men get more quickly rich, and sometimes more quickly poor, than at home. But, make no mistake, Jesse, people have to work and save in Australia, just as they have everywhere else, if they want to get on in the world. If they only want to live, perhaps it's easier there for the present.'

So we were not likely to believe these silly romancings, and warned the others not to mind them. But they would not listen to us. It would be, 'Mr. Jackson, the quartermaster says, that there was a girl came out last voyage but one in his ship that married a merchant within a month, and drove down in her own carriage to hire a servant the next ship that came in.'

'It MAY be true, but is far from likely,' we told her. 'You had better turn over in your own mind whether you would like to take a housemaid's or a laundress's place, which will be more to the purpose.'

But they couldn't help taking the brighter side, so poor silly things they dressed themselves in their most fashionable clothes when the ship was passed by the health officer, and went ashore with great expectations of offers of marriage and a life of ease.

As for Jane and me, we kept our best clothes in our boxes—not that we had many, and made ourselves so as to be ready for a journey, never doubting but that we should not be long in town. Before we landed we had time to look at Sydney Harbour, of which we'd heard such a lot from the sailors and some of the passengers that had been out before, and, my word! it was worth coming a long way to see.

I'm not much of a man for minding about scenery and all that. I've had my work to do, and other things to think about all my life. I daresay there's something in it, but it wasn't in my line, nor Jane's either much, but we couldn't help wondering at what a beautiful place it was.

We had come in a little after sunrise, and it was a bright clear day with scarce a ripple on the sea. It was the month of May, a winter month like November, but Lord! what a difference there was. The air was mild; the whole way from the Heads to the wharf—where we lay close to and could have touched, only they kept the ship out a bit, not to let people on board—was like a lake. On the shore, and on the heights above the dozens of little bays, nice gardens and white-walled houses and beautiful pine trees looked like gentlemen's parks and shrubberies in England. The sun seemed brighter, and the sky bluer, and the very sea-water clearer than on the other side of the world. Ships and steamers, yachts and pleasure boats, filled the harbour.

'Oh! what a lovely land!' said Jane, 'it's

like a place in a story-book; I feel sure we shall have good fortune here, if we deserve it.'

So we said good-bye to the captain and the doctor, and the officers, who all wished us luck, and said we'd be sure to get on. We were quite fond of the old ship that had carried us so safe; and Jane got her five pounds, and so we went off in good spirits to the Immigration Barracks.

Here we were all called by name, and had to answer to them before the Immigration Agent, who was very kind. Then the matron, a nice motherly woman, told all the single girls to go into one large room; the single men and boys into another; the married people into another. The public weren't allowed in till a certain hour, to prevent bustle and confusion. We were asked if we had friends expecting us. Of course we answered with the others. So Jane and I, and those that said their friends were to meet them, were put into a smaller room near the big outer gate.

Then a bell rang, and the friends were let in. How some of the immigrants looked and looked, as if they would know those they hadn't seen for years—some they'd never seen! Some found their friends at once, and went away with them joyfully. Others waited and waited, but no friends came. They looked very miserable, and more than one poor girl began to cry when the hours passed and no one came.

We weren't likely to do that. I had Mr. Buffray's letter and the address of his agent in my pocket, so I knew I could find him, and knew how to get on; but I thought we would wait till dinner-time, anyhow.

About twelve o'clock, the big clock was just striking when a busy-looking man bustled into the Immigration Barracks where we were waiting. He looked sharply round. 'Any one of the name of Jesse Claythorpe here?' he said, 'also Jane Claythorpe.'

I walked forward. 'We have been waiting for you, sir,' I said. 'Mr. Buffray told us that he would write to a friend to meet us.

He looked keenly at me, up and down, for a minute before he answered. 'Yes, yes! should have been here before, but went out of town last night. Vessel not expected in before this evening. And this is your sister! Had a pleasant voyage? Think you shall like the country?'

'I can't say yet, sir,' she answered. 'I've not seen anything but the harbour, which is wonderful.'

'Right to be cautious, quite right,' said the gentleman. 'Now I'm to send both of you to Mr. Buffray's place up the country, a long way off. Think you'll like that, eh?'

'We're used to the country, sir,' I said. 'I know Mr. Buffray pretty well. I was in his hunting stable at Applegate. When shall we have to start?'

'Hunting stable, eh? Buffray's doing it grand in England, I expect. Wool going down, too; but that's not my business. Well, say to-morrow morning. Must have a day to look round, eh?'

'We shall be quite ready, sir,' said Jane. 'One day will do for sight-seeing. How do we go? Is it very far?'

'Only about two hundred and fifty miles.' (Here Jane couldn't help giving a start.)

I said, 'That's a long way, sir. I suppose it's a little wild or so. But, anyhow, if it's good enough for Mr. Buffray and his wife and children, it's good enough for us, isn't it, Jane?'

'Of course,' she said. 'I was very foolish to think of the distance. But it seemed such a way off to English people. How do we travel?'

'You're a sensible girl,' he says, 'and you'll find it all right when you get there. Well, I'll send a cab for you and your boxes at six this evening to bring you to my house, where you'll stay to-night. To-morrow morning at seven o'clock the train starts. It takes you most of the way. The rest you do by coach. I'll arrange tickets, and all that. Now, good-bye till I see you again. My name's Nicholls, Albert Street, Redfern. Here's my card. Look at that if you're lost.'

We felt quite cheered up and confident after seeing Mr. Nicholls, I remember. We ate our dinner in the big room with the others, and had a talk about those that had gone and those that had stayed. There was some fun, too, about the girls that wouldn't take good offers at first, and wanted higher wages, or places as companions, or nursery governesses. People laughed at them, and passed on. Most of the best situations in the fine houses and gentlefolks' places were filled up at once, and at last these silly girls had to take what they could get, and be content with lower wages and less comfortable places. But they all agreed it was a wonderful town for servants, and that what would be high wages at home was thought nothing of here. Very few questions were asked either as to whether they were good at this or that work. The great thing was whether they were willing, and would promise to do their best. This showed how scarce servants must have been compared to England.

After dinner we took a walk round the beautiful park, the Botanical Garden as they called it, which Jane said made her think of the Garden of Eden in the Bible. After that we walked down the main streets, George Street and Pitt Street, and looked at the shops and went into the fruit market, where we were surprised to see apples and pears, with oranges, bananas, pine-apples, and other strange fruits in piles and cart-loads.

The shops, Jane said, must be nearly as fine as those in London—the drapers, and jewellers, and hardware very particularly. Then about four in the afternoon the street began to fill with carriages, with fine ladies, and coachmen, and footmen, going into the shops and walking about on the pavements just the same as at home. Some of the horses were grand, high-conditioned, and well turned-out. No wonder Mr. Buffray had learned to ride in a country so full of fine horses.

'Why, Jane,' I said, 'this is England over again, isn't it? though this is a different town from poor old Applegate or Westerham either. But look at the cabs, the omnibuses, the carts, the trollies—everything, talk and all, just like what we've left. Why do people make such a fuss about coming to a country like this?'

'Because they don't know any better,' she said. 'Oh! Jesse, think of what it might have been for father and poor mother if they'd had the luck to come here like Stephen Buffray?'

'Or plenty of other people,' I said. 'But we can't help it, Jane. We have got here ourselves, that's something. But I'd live on bread and water for years to come if it would only put mother alongside of us in this beautiful bright country.'

'I thought there were no beggars here,' said Jane, wiping the tears out of her eyes; 'but there's one with a card round his neck, blind, poor fellow.' So she dropped a penny into his plate among the silver that was there.

It made a great noise, and the beggar thought it was a half-crown or a florin, as he took it up and began, 'Lord bless and keep ye, my pretty miss.' He could tell it was a woman's foot and voice. It's wonderful how sharp blind people get. For the same reason he knew by the touch of the coin that it was a penny. His face changed, and he stopped in the middle of his blessing, and growled out something that sounded just the opposite.

'There's an Australian beggar for you,' I said, laughing at Jane's look of surprise and pain. 'He doesn't care for coppers. Look at the sixpences and threepenny bits in his plate. There's a shilling, too. No wonder he thinks your penny spoils the look of it all.'

'He's an ungrateful old wretch,' said Jane. She hated waste and extravagance, did sister Jane. 'He deserves to want if anybody ever does in this rich place.'

Rich! well, it looked so to us. All the people—though, of course, there were rich and poor, as you might say—were well-dressed, happy, and prosperous looking. The horses were all well fed and with shining coats. You saw no people with patched clothes, and the look that poverty and uncertainty about to-morrow's bread writes in large hand on people's faces. No; every one seemed happy and contented. Even the blind man had a clean shirt, a warm coat, and new boots. No wonder he couldn't afford to be civil for a penny.

CHAPTER V

MR. J. ROPER, OF YUGILDAH

WE hadn't half the trouble we'd thought about in getting up to Bandra, Jane and I. We went most of the way by rail and coach, and then a 'jackaroo' met us with a fine pair of horses in a waggonette. I expected to see a first cousin to a kangaroo when the coach-driver told us, instead of a young gentleman learning squatting, and a manly pleasant young fellow he was.

When we got to the station it was all plain sailing. Jane thought the missis the nicest lady she ever met, and she was very glad to see Jane, as they hadn't had a housemaid for a month. So they got to be quite friendly like, and she told every one Jane was a treasure.

I had a pair of carriage horses and one or two other nags, besides three or four vehicles, to clean and see to. The stable was nearly as full as the Squire's, and I soon showed the overseer that I meant work and could do it. Then they had races, and I won the big handicap at the township with Tornado, an old favourite horse of Mr. Buffray's, and every one said it was very easy seen I'd learned to ride in good company. All the work came easy. Jane and I were as happy as the day was long. And after a bit the master came out from England.

After he'd been home a bit I'd found out that keeping on being a groom and coachman wasn't the way people made their money in this country. I wanted to tackle something bigger, and more likely to grow into property. I had heard lots of stories from the youngsters about this man and that beginning with a few cattle or sheep, and now being worth thousands.

So I made up my mind to get away to one of the far-off stations as soon as I could, and as there was a lot of colts going to be sent to Yugildah—a 'run' on the plains down the river—I made bold to ask Mr. Buffray to let me take them there, and have the job of breaking them in. He wasn't best pleased at first, but after a bit he said I was quite right to try and better myself, and he'd give me the driving and breaking.

So I said good-bye to Jane, who couldn't help crying at the thought of my going so far, but said I was acting right; and off I started in a day or two, with a boy to help drive and a pack-horse, as pleased as Punch. When I got up to the 'back station' at Yugildah, as it was called, I was struck all of a heap with the look of the place. It happened to be a hottish day, though it was only early summer, and I thought it was worse than anything we'd had last year at Bandra.

There was something about the whole affair that seemed to me not only wild and outlandish, but dismal looking. I drove up my horses, put 'em in the stock-yard, and fastened up the slip-rails, and then we rode down to the huts. There were three of them altogether, two of 'em by the side of an ugly creek with steep banks, so straight down that the cook had a kind of arrangement—a bucket that slipped along a wire rope, and was drawn up by a windlass—to get water with.

There was no garden, no stable—nothing but a tumble-down two-railed horse paddock. The only good improvement was a big cattle yard—strong enough for wild elephants. Where the huts were had once been covered with trees, but most of them had been cut down, and only their stumps left. Plains all round and everywhere, like the sea.

I'd had my dinner, and was sitting on a bench outside the hut feeling a bit better, when I saw two men and a black boy riding across the plain. 'Here comes Mr. Roper,' said Jack, the cook. 'They've been at Mildool muster.' 'Which is him?' says I. 'The one in the front riding the big bay horse. That's Quondong—the best hack and stock-horse in these parts. He can walk as fast as some horses can trot, cut out any beast that ever stood on a camp, and canter round a cheese plate.' This was a bit of a blow, but when I saw him come tearing along with his head up—doing at square walk, and no amble, a good five miles an hour—I found they'd some smart horses as well as men in these parts.

The overseer, when he came close, turned

out to be a tall, hard-faced, dried-up looking man, that looked as if living in that hot country had shrivelled all the sap out of him. He was a native-born Australian, and had come up as a boy from Penrith, where he was reared. He'd lived for twenty years or more on this very place. He had pretty near lost his eyesight with the sandy blight, which made him put his head forward when he spoke, as if he took you for some one else, or was looking for what he couldn't find. Anyway he was given in to be one of the best bushmen in that part of the country: the men said he could find his way over it blindfold, or the darkest night that ever was. Roper rode easy and light in his saddle, though he was a tall man; but there was that sort of look about him as he sat there that I've seen with many a man in this country, as if he'd been born on a horse, and was ten times as much at home in a saddle as on a chair or his own legs.

He rides up to the door of the hut and dismounts, pulls off his saddle and bridle, and lets his horse go before he says a word. Then he looks at me sharp, pushing his head forward and blinking his eyes, and says, 'You're the young chap the boss sent out from the old country. I heard you was coming up with them horses. You've got a letter or something, I suppose, for me.' I handed him the letter. 'Yes, yes!' he says, after making believe to read it all careful. 'Your name Claythorpe—Jesse Claythorpe! I thought that was a woman's name. Never heard of a man being called so.'

'Ever hear of any one called David, the son of Jesse, in the Old Testament?' says I, rather hasty like.

'Can't say as I remember,' says he. 'We haven't had a Bible in this place this years. Had to send a policeman twenty miles for one the last inquest the coroner held here. So his father's name was Jesse, was it! Well I'll take your word for it, young man. And now we'll go down to the yard and count out the horses. They can stay in the paddock till sundown. I'll yard and tail 'em after to-morrow—till they get used to the run a bit. They'd make straight back for Bandra if we were to let 'em go now. You're to begin breaking 'em in, the boss says.'

'How am I to do that without a stable?' says I.

'Haven't you got a first-rate yard?' says he, 'and a paddock—what more d'ye want? a bloomin' circus, eh? Many a good colt I've broken without so much as a paddock. Turned 'em out every night, and tied 'em up with a green-hide rope to a tree, when they wanted lunging. Old Quondong was broke that way, and where's there a hack like him on the river?'

'That's not my style,' says I. 'It's a handy way to kill a good young 'un or two as would pay for a middlin' stable. But I suppose I must do the best I can. I didn't come all this way to grumble.'

'That's the way to look at it,' says he, growing a bit civiller. 'You'll get colonised after a bit, like all the rest of us.'

'I daresay,' says I, passing it off, though I didn't mean it all the same. 'Is there a lad in the place I can have to help me catch the horses and tackle them. The young chap that came with me is going back, and it's awkward work by oneself.'

'There's a darkie, a chap that was dropped

sick by the drover of the last mob of cattle that passed through from Queensland. He's a sulky cove, but he can ride. Talgai! come here, you black sweep. Look alive or I'll freshen you up with my stock-whip.'

The boy walked over, not much quicker for Roper's bullying. He was heavy made and awkward for a black fellow, but he looked us straight in the face, and didn't seem cowed. He'd a good eye in his head, too. I thought he was about eighteen from the hair on his face, but I believe now he was younger.

'There,' says Roper, 'here he is, and I'll sell him to you out and out. I gave Benson £5 for the chance of him. He's worth more, but you can have him for the same money. I knew he couldn't be much good, or he'd never have left him behind, though he looked more dead than alive. *I* can't knock anything out of him. I'd a dashed-fine mind to shoot him one day. Still he might suit you.'

'I'll take him. We'll get on without the gun,' says I.

'I don't know about that, but lay the whip into him well if you'll take my tip. I never saw a black fellow yet that would work without it. You hear—you bull-pup—Jesse, here, knock devil out of you 'spose you no burra burri like't white fellow.'

The boy looked at me like a pointer pup that thinks the keeper's whip's coming; but I laughed and said, 'Now you blackfellow you belongy me, allysame hut-keeper. Come along and boilem kettle 'longa supper.'

I knew that I was to have a hut to myself. It was farther along the creek. Not a very grand one, but there were two rooms in it, and a pretty good chimney, with a bed and slab table. I intended to make it snug. I liked the notion of being by myself, and not in the men's hut, or with the overseer. There was a skillion behind, which could be filled up with a bunk for Talgai. He could look after things when I was out. The first colt to be broke in was Talgai himself. I could see he hadn't been well handled. He'd been hammered and sworn at and bullied by the men he'd been with, and as he was a game sort of pup, with more 'bull' in him than blacks mostly have, it made him sulky, and put vice into his head. So I set to work to fetch him round a bit. He was fond of smoking—nearly all blacks are, and why shouldn't they? They've a deal of time on their hands when you come to think of it, and if it makes the hours pass pleasant, when they can't read or haven't their own people to talk to, why not? It doesn't shorten their lives that I've ever seen; and if it did, why—no great matter either. So I gave him a fig of tobacco to start with. I'd learned to smoke regular myself by this time, and when evening came set him to boil the kettle while I fished out the beef and bread, and pannikins, and tea and sugar that the cook had put in a kind of rough cupboard for me. The overseer told him. After a bit the tea was made, and Talgai took his bread and beef, and sat on a log outside. I took my meal in the hut, but we'd both the same kind of tucker. I was just thinking the place was awful rough, when all of a sudden it came into my heart about how many times Jane and I had hardly a bit of bread to put in our mouths in the old country, much less meat; and the weather that cold and dismal it was enough to starve us to death. Then I thought of the plentifulness of everything, and the good wages here. If there WAS a little roughing, we were both young, and could stand it. Not that Jane had any; she had a regular lady's life of it, as she often said. 'It would be a cowardly thing to grumble now, and ungrateful to boot,' I said almost out loud. 'Besides I'm going to be a man or a mouse one of these days yet.'

Just then Talgai, who had been lighting his pipe—a very black clay—begins all of a sudden. 'What name belongin' to you? That one Roper always yabber like't swearum.'

'My name is Jesse,' says I; 'Jesse Claythorpe.'

'Jess-ee, Jess-ee,' he says pretty slow. 'Me Minālee. That one boss belongin' to me at Bundaberg win two fellow race alonga big mare Jess-see. Baal whitefellow name that one!'

I saw I couldn't make him understand that there was a man's name and a woman's with the same sound. He was puzzled, and gave it up.

'Me callum you mahmee (master) that

best fella,' he said, so we settled it at that.

I told him to bring his blankets into the skillion and settle up his bunk, and most of next day I spent in making the hut clean and comfortable, putting up pegs for saddles and bridles, and making everything ship-shape. I never could abear muddling and untidy ways, and I can't now, for the life of me. There's no groom worth his salt that isn't neat in his ways, nor no stable fit to call one where the boys ain't brought up to put everything in its place, and be as regular as clockwork. The very horses like it, and thrive as well again for knowing the hour and minute they'll get their food and exercise, day after day.

When we'd finished, and it took us to dark, the hut looked quite different. I'd made Talgai sweep all the front and rake up the chips, and burn them and the rubbish, and with a bit of a clear wood fire burning in the evening I sat down on one end of the stool, and thought myself quite grand. I got out my pen and ink, and wrote a letter to Jane, for I knew she'd be uneasy till she heard how I was getting on.

Talgai sat outside for more than an hour, smoking, over the fire he'd made of the rubbish heap, when all of a sudden he says,

'Mahmee; You buy me along of that one Roper?'

'No good that one, Talgai,' I said.

'Big one whitefellow put me alonga chokee; that one Benson sell me alonga Roper!' he went on quite seriously, 'big one sore longa cobra; big one me sick. Mine think it go along a ground, and jump up white fella. Me hear'um Benson, say, "I'll take five pounds." That one Roper yabber all right, "me gibit, five note and chance it."'

'Then that one Benson laugh, and ride away after cattle. Suppose black boy die, he no care. Long time me very bad, like't here (then he put his hand on his chest and head), all right now. That one Roper yabber me got pleuro, you think um pleuro?' And he looked at me quite pitiful like.

'Not a bit of it,' says I. 'You're all right now. You got big one cold, like that one colt got strangles; all right now, by and by you grow up big fellow.'

His eyes fairly brightened up; the poor fellow thought he was going to die, and that made him so dozy and stupid like. He'd seen many a one of his countrymen die the same way. They get wet travelling with stock, and take no care of themselves, catch a heavy cold, it settles on the chest, and soon makes an end of them.

I could see he'd taken a fancy to me now, and I knew if so be I got regularly master of him he'd be worth two white boys. He'd do what I told him about the horses, and not be too conceited to learn, which is everything with a youngster.

Next day we had breakfast early, ran the horses up out of the paddock into the yard, and made a beginning. There were some small yards, and a 'crush,' as they call it, for branding cattle. I drafted off four of the colts and a couple of quiet horses. I wouldn't let Talgai rope them, as he wanted to—he was very smart at that; but we managed with a good deal of patience and humbugging to halter two, and get the tackle on them. Then we let them walk about the yard and exercise themselves, champing the bit, and all that. We caught them again at dinner time, and stroked them over, trying to make them know we weren't going to hurt them. My line in breaking horses is to be as quiet and as kind as you can with them from the first, never to be sudden or harsh with them, or to lose patience. They're only babies after all; of course like with children you must be firm, and show you're not frightened of 'em. And there ARE bad-tempered ones among all lots of horses, it's bred in 'em—same as in men and women. You must take THEM easy too, bullying makes 'em worse. They'll never be any chop perhaps, but if *kindness won't fetch 'em nothing will*, take my tip for that, and I've tried both ways. At night we turned 'em into the paddock, and pretty stiff and sore they must have felt, poor things. Next day we caught two more, I went steadily on by degrees with the whole lot. Talgai was a first-class rough-rider, and could sit anything.

He was inclined to be hard on them, like all lads, black or white—but when he saw I wouldn't have it, he left it off, and did what I told him.

When the mob was finished the overseer said they were the best broken-in lot of colts he'd ever seen in that part of the country. He praised me up in his rough way, and spoke so kind to Talgai that the poor chap would have blushed if he'd a skin that showed it.

I'd worked pretty hard at the horses, and thought I was due for a change. So I asked Roper if there wasn't anything about the cattle that I could manage. I didn't want to be idle, and the horses would stay as they were for a while.

'There's some cattle to be fetched from one of the back runs on Murdering Creek—Boree they call it,' he said. 'About two hundred. They went back there last winter. There's a man out there that'll help you part of the way in. There's no road, and a point of scrub to get through. I don't know how you'll make out the line. Oh! I forgot; Talgai can go with you. He was there once, so of course he knows the road again. These niggers never forget THAT.'

This was the very thing I wanted. I began to think breaking-in horses was very well in its way, but that I'd never make my fortune out of that line of business, besides the chance of getting my leg broke, or neck, indeed. With young horses the best man may come on an accident, and more than one young fellow I've known finished up that could ride anything, and by no fault of his own either. So you young fellows don't be too proud of your riding. You might be crippled or killed outright any day.

So we started away next day as jolly as sandboys. Stock-whips we had too. Talgai had managed to smuggle an old gun, which he put on the pack horse. 'Me seeum wild duck, big fellow wild turkey, I believe,' he said, 'longa Old Man Plain.' So I let him bring it.

We started at sunrise, and when we got outside of the station track, Talgai made as straight as a line for the north-west, and kept to one point of the compass, I could see, without even a twist or a turn. I've seen a black boy do that in country where he'd never been before, when they only told him the direction, and he stuck to it after dark too, and brought his party straight to the station they were going to. They're wonderful people that way—beat us whites hollow. But sometimes they get frightened and lose their heads. Then it's all up with them, and they're useless.

We camped about 12 o'clock by a creek, where we tethered one horse and let the others go in hobbles. It was a pretty place though wild and solitary; but when the tea boiled I thought the beef and damper tasted better than anything I'd ever eaten. By and by we tackled up again and rode on till sundown.

Then we came to an out-station of one of the neighbours, a miserable old hut it was, with only a stockman and a hut-keeper. They were both rough, dirty-looking fellows, and I'd far rather have camped under a tree, but there was a paddock for the horses, and that made a difference. However, I told Talgai we wouldn't do it coming back.

It's a curious thing how little some of the old-fashioned squatters ever did in the way of improvements. There was a grand run, and a fine herd of cattle. The owners—old Sydney-side people—lived in town. They'd had it thirty or forty years, and the slab hut, a stockyard, and paddock were all the buildings they'd ever put up, though they must have taken thousands of pounds off it.

I heard a story about these two men, the stockman and hut-keeper that lived there, that wasn't bad in its way. A surveyor happened to call at the place, and both of them were out—the stockman after cattle, and the hut-keeper over at the next station. He expected to get something to eat, and to be shown the way. He didn't manage either, as the place was so filthy dirty that he couldn't touch anything. He happened to know their names, and, being a bit of a card, he wrote on the door with a piece of chalk—

"Dick and Bob, of Yalco-green,
Are the dirtiest pair that ever were seen."

'Dirty Dick,' as he was called, came home an hour or so afterwards, and saw by the horse tracks that a white man had been to the hut. He also saw the writing on the door. Now at this time he was expecting the master on one of his half-yearly visits. He couldn't read, neither could Bob. He began to think, indeed to be fully sure, that his master had come, and gone away again for a day or two to a neighbouring station, and that the strange letters on the door were about his making a muster and getting all the herd 'on camp' without loss of time. Such an order meant sending word round to all the neighbours, as of course a single pair, even if Bob left the hut to itself and went with them, could not do much by themselves with two thousand head of cattle.

After thinking it over for nearly an hour, it struck him that the only way to get at the sense of this writing was to carry it bodily to the nearest home station, where there would be sure to be some one who could read and write.

Dick was a strong wiry fellow, though soap and water wasn't much in his line, so he prises the door off its hinges,—they were only wooden (there was mighty little iron about a station in THOSE days)—bark and green hide, slabs let into grooves above and below, did the most of it,—claps it on to his back and starts off at a dog trot to do the twelve miles to the next station. A hardwood slab door weighs a goodish deal, as any one may find out that has to hump it a hundred yards. However, Dick was pretty tough, and as fit as regular exercise and beef and damper could make him. So he did the twelve miles in three hours or thereabouts, and trots in with his door on his back up to the men's hut of Mr. Lowe's home station.

When the cook saw him take the door off his back, and put it up against the kitchen, while he wiped his forehead with a big yellow silk handkerchief (the sort they used to work up for crackers in those days), he thought Dick had gone out of his mind, and started to run over to the house. But Dick muzzled him, and gave him a volley or two, just to show he was sensible like.

'What blamed foolishness are you up to? Is the cove at home?'

'He's over at the house, but what do yer mean by roofin' over yer back with twenty-feet of hardwood like that? Are ye afraid of hailstorms or is it too hot for yer, or what is it? Have ye had a keg up on the quiet?'

'You tell Mr. Lowe that Yalco-green Dick wants to see him, and don't stand chattering and opening yer head like a laughing jackass. He'll know when he sees me. I'm not off my chump, no more than you are, and I haven't smelt spirits since last Christmas.'

'And then you went in a docker, eh, Dick? But here's the master coming, and you can pitch your own yarn to him.'

'Well, Dick,' said Mr. Lowe—a good-natured gentleman he was, 'cattle all right? Not branded any of my calves lately? I suppose you are out of tea and sugar. I can lend you some till the drays come up.'

"'Taint nothing o' that sort, Mr. Lowe,' says Dick, grinning. 'As to the calves, I'm a few short myself, as I think that half-caste chap of yours must have "duffed." But I want you to read this here writin', if you'll be good enough. Ye see I'm expectin' the master, and I don't know the day he'll be here.' As he says this he lifts the door up, and holds it before Mr. Lowe.

'Is it anything about the master, sir, or when the cattle's to be drafted? I'm short of horses too, now Whitefoot's gone lame.'

Mr. Lowe cast his eye over the bit of poetry, and all but burst out laughing in Dick's anxious face. He stopped himself however.

'It isn't anything about the cattle, Dick,' he says, 'I am very sorry you have had the long walk over for nothing.'

'Walk be dashed!' says Dick; 'a few miles is neither here nor there. I'm just as well pleased it ain't a general muster. Who wrote it, and wot does he say?'

It was Mr. Langley, the surveyor, and this is what he wrote, and the whole female population (Mr. Lowe was a married man) had gathered up to hear the fun. Then Mr. Lowe read it out—

> 'Dick and Bob, of Yalco-green,
> Are the dirtiest pair that ever were seen.'

'Well, I'm blowed!' says Dick, 'and to think of my carrying the bloomin' thing every step of the way here for that. It's twelve mile, sir, every inch of it. I'm jiggered if I carry it back again though, if the blessed hut never has a door again. There'll be a dray coming over some day.'

'And I'll see that it goes back safe,' said Mr. Lowe, after every one had done laughing. 'It's an interesting document though. If I could I would have a photo taken of it.'

CHAPTER VI

MR. BURDOCK, OF WALLANBAH

WE were finishing up the third day, and I was wondering whether the plain would ever come to an end, when Talgai sings out 'Wagh!' and pointed with his chin, like all blacks do. I looked and looked, but deuce a thing could I see. At last I made out a whirlwind coming our way. When it came closer it turned out to be a run-away horse in a buggy. On he came, a fine-looking bay horse in good condition, at a pretty smart gallop. He had a buggy behind him, with the hood all on one side, and he making it rattle like a canister tied to a dog's tail. The splash board was stove in, but there wasn't much chance of its being upset, as there were no stumps, and not a tree within five miles; still it jumped up into the air, and swung about every now and then, as if a little would make it capsize. We rode at the horse, as soon as he passed us, from different sides. I got him by the head, and we managed to stop him between us. He was reg'lar set up, and pulled hard at first, but got quiet to lead after a bit. I made Talgai go ahead and follow the back tracks, which of course he could do easy enough, though I couldn't see half a mark on the baked dry soil.

After going about three miles, Talgai pointed to a dark object at the edge of the plain; what it was I could not make out. 'That one Mahmee bin fall out alonga buggy I believe,' says he.

When we got nearer to one another, a stout-built elderly man comes towards us, not very fast, for he was lame, but he got on as well as he could. 'That one, Mr. Burdock, big one Mahmee—live along Wallanbah.'

When he came up, Mr. Burdock very soon explained all about himself and the horse too.

'By ——' he said, 'young man, you've

done me a good turn to-day. I don't know who you are, but I'll do you another if ever I get the chance. Blast that infernal horse! A goanna started him, and he set to and kicked the front of the buggy in—pretty near broke my leg and chucked me out over a yarran stump. I'm blessed if I could have walked home, and what I'd have done if you hadn't stopped him I don't know. Who do you belong to, Billy?'

'Me, Talgai—longa Yugildah.'

'By George! I remember you now. You're Benson's boy that was took sick when the cattle passed. Thought you was dead long ago. Tell ye what, both on ye, come back to Wallanbah to-night and go on in the morning. What's your name, young man? I suppose you're one of Buffray's mob?'

'My name's Claythorpe; came from Bandra with horses; I'm going over to Back Boree for some cattle that got away from Yugildah last winter.'

'I know, I know,' he says. 'There's no calves among 'em or Roper 'd had 'em back months ago. Smart cove, he is, Master Jim

Roper. Well, you come home with me, and I'll send my stockman, Jack Hall, with you, and he shall give you a hand part of the way back. What d'ye say?'

It wasn't far out of our way, and we was not pushed for time. His man would be a great help, for I didn't know the country, of course. I said yes, so we held the horse while he got in, and then we all started at a rattling pace across the plain. His horse had got some of the fight knocked out of him, and didn't want to kick any more. We got on a track after a bit, and made Wallanbah, which was a big comfortable-looking head station, before dark.

'You go alonga men's hut, Talgai, first time, yarraman yan likeit big one paddock,' says Mr. Burdock, giving the buggy to a couple of young fellows that ran out from the stables, 'and you come into the house, Claythorpe, so as you and me can have a yarn comfortable.'

I followed him into the house, which was a large, rambling, shingled cottage, built of pine let into grooved uprights, plastered and lined inside. 'Here's a bedroom,' he says;

'put your things in there, and come into the parlour. My wife and daughters are all away in Sydney; and now I think a glass of brandy and water won't hurt us after all that smash and run-away business. *I* want something, I know.'

I wouldn't take any. He helped himself to a 'third mate's glass,' and took a good pull. 'You don't touch, I see. Well, this is a free country. Every man does what he likes best in my house; and I don't say you're wrong, mind you. If I was to tell you of all the men I've seen go to the bad since I've been on Wallanbah—good fellows too—it would frighten you. I take it because I like it, and I can pull up when I've had enough. But many a man can't. That's why I don't care to see a youngster take to it like mother's milk. It's a bad sign. Here's the tea a-comin' in; that'll be more in your line. Take a look at them oranges in the garden (I've got a pump as brings the water up from the creek), and by that time we'll have something before us.'

A clean-looking old woman brought in tea. After a couple of days' camping out I had something like an appetite for it. Hot mutton chops, potatoes, and cabbage with lettuce and cress afterwards, and first-rate butter. It was prime. Milk and butter were never seen at Yugildah; no vegetables neither, not so much as a potato. They wouldn't be bothered to milk a cow; lived like blackfellows, as the saying is.

After tea we sat outside on the verandah, and had a smoke. It was fine and cool, and the garden put me in mind of the pleasant times at Bandra. Mr. Burdock took another glass of brandy and water. He talked quite free and pleasant, and got me to tell him how I came out to Australia. 'So that was it,' he says, after I'd done. 'You did the right thing in coming out here, you may take your oath of that. I'm a different man to-day from what I'd ha' been if I'd stopped in the blessed Old Country, that's so chock full of chaps like you and me that one's taking the bread out of the other's mouth, and jolly nigh starved at that. I made the place too hot to hold me, for I was rather rombustious as a youngster, and might have been sent out at the Queen's expense, only

I had just sense enough to run away to sea, where I had the life and soul pretty near licked out of me before we got into Sydney Harbour. Then I had that good judgment that I ran away again, stowed myself away in a crib in the Rocks, and then made up into the bush, the best day's work ever I did— THAT was.'

Here the old chap took a pull at his brandy and water, filled his pipe again, and settled down steady like for a tough yarn.

'I asked for work at the first station I came to, and though I was strange to it, I wired in with a will and took things as they came. The grub was A1 after ship biscuit and junk, and a lad that had had the third mate after him with a rope's end half his time, night and day, wasn't likely to turn up his nose at shore work. As a west country chap we had used to say, "I've allays been used to slaving, and I do'ant expect now't else." Sailors are the best men at any kind of bush work. They're able to turn their hands to anything, and they've been broke in to obey orders, and no two ways about it. I've had soldiers as wasn't bad, but in a general way they're no chop. I saved my money and lived close for years. After a bit, when I had knocked about over one shearing, I made as good a "rouse-about" as here and there one. I earned my pound a week easy, and took to the bush for good and all. I'd a decentish headpiece, too, though if I'd stayed in England I shouldn't have had much of a show for using it. I "knocked down" my money like the rest for a year or two, till I began to cipher up a bit whether I couldn't save my wages and start a bit of a station on my own hook.'

'That takes money,' I said.

'Not so much in them days, and it's to be done NOW without such a lot of cash, if a man only goes about it the right way. Anyhow, I saw men doing a stroke with cattle and sheep of their own that I knew hadn't hardly a five pound note to start with. So I reckoned I'd have a try myself when I could muster the cash.'

'But that's the hard part of it,' says I, listening with all my might to see what I could pick up, for I saw it was as good a chance as I should have to find out how to climb fortune's ladder. Old Mr. Burdock finished his second tumbler, and began to mix a third. It didn't seem to have no effect on him. It doesn't on some men, here and there. Then he lit his pipe and went on again.

'Somehow it came into my head that shepherds seemed to save more money than any other of the station hands. They had their cheques at the end of the year, and one or two as I knew had money in the bank. Most of 'em blued theirs in the first public-house they met. But I wasn't going for that foolishness no longer.'

'So the first chance I got I took a flock of sheep at Buckajinga, because I knew I should live at an out-station, with an old card they called Sails, that I'd cottoned to somehow. He'd been a man-o'-warsman as had voyaged all round the world, and was as good as a book to talk to. He'd a fancy for me because I'd been at sea, so I thought we'd get on well together.'

'How long were you shepherding, then?' says I.

'Two year,' says the old chap, 'two

mortal long twelve months. One thing I wanted to get hold of, that was the lay of the country. Old Sails, as they called him, he'd been sail-maker in the *Dido*, knew every run from here to the Queensland border, and would pitch about them by the hour. He'd a good notion of the points of the compass and the distance between one run and another. He was book-learned pretty fair, and made me read the paper we took in out loud to him. It was a weekly one, and as we were allowed to kill our own sheep once a fortnight, we had plenty of fat to make candles. The sheep had any amount of feed, and gave no trouble to speak of. It wasn't a bad sort of life, I can tell you.'

'I daresay not,' I says, 'but wasn't it very lonely and dull?'

'Not so bad as you'd think. I got used to it after a month or two, though we never saw a soul but the ration-carrier and the overseer, perhaps once in three months. The seasons was better long ago—more grass and water everywhere—not so many sheep either; that made a deal of difference.'

'One day the old man says to me, "Look

here, Sam," says he, "I see by this paper that Buckajo is to be sold. The cove's outrun the constable, and Richard Jones and Co. are a going to sell him up. Now everything's desperate low, and cash is that scarce they're glad to take it for anything. It's my belief that they'd sell a flock of ewes for half-a-crown or three shillings a head, and give in this out-station, Buckajinga. I've got betwixt two and three hundred in the bank, and you've about seventy or eighty. What do you say to making a dart for it?"

'And one day, to make a long story short, I bought twelve hundred ewes for three-and-sixpence a head, cash down, and the out-station Buckajinga given in. Of course, it was dirt cheap, but squatters, and merchants too, was short of cash in those days, and my money was there, without expense or commission. That's where it was. All the pots and buckets and hut and hurdles were given in too. That saved a few pounds.'

'Then you got a station and a flock of breeding ewes,' I said, 'and everything that you wanted, all for two hundred and ten pounds. That seems cheap enough.'

'It WAS cheap, no two ways about that, and it was the start of a pretty big pile; still it was the market price. If they'd driven the sheep to Sydney, they mightn't have fetched half-a-crown. There's no chances like that now. But money's to be made yet, for all that.'

'I'd like to know the way,' says I. 'I've saved every penny I've earned since I came out, except what's gone in clothes and tobacco, but I didn't see any way of trading with it.'

'Saved your money, have you?' says the old chap, looking at me as if he'd see through me and half way into the wall on the other side. 'Well, you're one of the right sort. Don't you never go for to drink no grog, neither. It's a bad line for a young feller; once you start on it, ten to one you can't pull up again; I'm turned seventy, and I know what I can stand and what I can't, so I take my grog free and cheerful, if I've a friend with me. But I've seen many a fine young chap, as was strong and plucky, and well eddicated, and belonged to a tip-top family to boot, go down to the lowest through drink; yes, so that he'd beg a drink or a shilling from a travelling tinker. And now it's a fair thing for bed. I'll send Jack with you to-morrow, and you come back this way and stop a night. We'll have another yarn, and I might lay you on to something.'

We shook hands, and Mr. Burdock walked off to bed, steady enough, though he'd had three or four stiffish glasses of grog. But he could stand a lot. I've seen a few men like that; but for one that holds up, makes money, and keeps his health, there's a hundred goes down.

CHAPTER VII

MISS POSSIE BARKER, OF BOREE

I WAS up at daylight and roused out Talgai to bring up the horses. It ain't often a blackfellow 'll get up without calling, even the best of 'em. Early as it was Mr. Burdock was up too, walking about in his shirt sleeves and looking as fresh as if he'd camped out with nothing stronger to drink than quart-pot tea.

'Nothin' beats an early start,' says he, 'breakfast 'll be ready by the time you've saddled up and packed. Don't you forget what I said last night. You'll lose nothing by coming this way, it's a few miles round, but a stockyard's everything with cattle just off their beat.'

I was pretty sure not to forget to come by Wallanbah; the quarters were too good.

I said, anyhow, we were not pushed for a day or two, and there was nothing much to do when we got back to Yugildah.

'It's a rough shop, ain't it? and Roper's a rum chap when his monkey's up. I don't go there now; we had a barney about some calves. He bested me then, but he'll land himself in the logs about that same calf racket if he doesn't look out, some day.'

'Logs!' I says. 'There don't seem to be many about this part. The trees are all too small. I should think the yard at Yugildah is strong enough to brand all the calves on the run in a month.'

He laughed. 'You don't tumble quite,' he says. 'It don't matter, either, it'll come by degrees. Tell your boy to saddle up and get his breakfast in the kitchen.'

'Look here, Claythorpe,' he says, after breakfast, 'don't you get collared on Poss Barker, she's a fine girl, but you'll do better than her if you mind yourself.'

'Who's Poss Barker?' says I. 'I began to think there were no women in these parts; and why shouldn't I get "collared," as you call it?'

'Well, she's George Barker's gal at Boree, and a fine upstanding filly to look at as ever you came across. He's had her eddicated; more's the pity. I think he'd better have let her grow up like her mother, and then she'd ha' been contented.'

'Education never hurt anybody,' says I, rather quick. 'Why should it be worse for her than for you and me?'

'Well, you'll see when you get there,' says the old chap, laughing to himself like. 'Poor Possie (that's short for Possum—she got the name when she was little, for being so soft-looking and bright about the eyes). I seen her turned out in a regular fine habit last time I was there mustering. She was riding old Cooramen, as won the Yanjee Town Plate two years ago. I was reg'lar stunned, but I say *take care of her*, that's all.' So we shook hands and away we started.

We got along first-rate with the Wallanbah stock-rider to show us the way. He was a smart young fellow, full of fun and tricks; he made his horse rear and kick, and played off a few jokes upon Talgai, which set me laughing. He could speak the blacks' language, and though Talgai came from a different part, he could make him understand. They had a deal of jokes between themselves. He was native-born, and so was his father, he told me. What he didn't know about horses and cattle wasn't much, and you couldn't put him wrong in the bush night or day, wet or dry.

He took the lead. Talgai and he understood one another, I could see, so I left em to fix it between themselves. Straight through scrub and forest, plain and creek, he went without seemingly studying anything. It was latish in the afternoon when we came in sight of the hut and yards.

'There's Back Boree,' says he; 'we'll be pretty comfortable to-night.'

'Why, it's a big place,' says I. 'I thought it was only an out-station.'

'I don't know as it's much more,' says Jack, 'but old Barker has a good-looking daughter, and a lot of kids. Possie's a smart girl, and keeps a better house than many a white woman.'

'Why, bless my heart! what colour is she?'

says I. 'I've seen never a woman at all in this part, and now you say she isn't white.'

'Well, she's betwixt and between. Poss is a half-caste, as the saying is. Her mother was a good-looking gin, and while she lived she kept old Barker pretty straight. He's a tiger to drink when the fit's on him.'

'And this girl, Possie as you call her, she's educated?'

'You'll see for yourself,' says he, laughing. 'I aint much in that line, but she's been to school in Bathurst, and so's the boy, young Johnny. There's the old man himself, and he'll know to a mile where them WG cattle runs.'

As we rode up to the biggest hut near the bank of the creek a tall heavy man walked towards us from the stock-yard, with a hide rope in his hand.

'Hallo! Jack,' he says to the stock-rider, 'what's up? We're not going to muster this month yet. Are you going to send away fat cattle, or what is it?'

'This is Mr. Claythorpe, from Yugildah,' says Jack. 'He's come over with the black boy to fetch them WG cattle that got away over here last year.'

'Oh, that's it,' says he. 'You're welcome Mr. Claythorpe. I thought Roper was going to leave 'em till they got fat, and send 'em down with our next lot. It's a pity to move 'em now, they're broke in like to the run. Come along in and stay the night; we can do nothing before the morning. I think the paddock's all right, but you'd better hobble your horse, Jack.'

We took off the saddles and put them on the verandah, which was pretty wide; then we let the horses go in the paddock. Talgai went into the kitchen, and Jack and I followed Barker into a snug enough sitting-room. As we opened the door, a tall girl rose up from a sofa covered with a rug made of a soft fur, something like sealskin, and smiled at Jack Hall.

'Possie, this is Mr. Claythorpe,' says the old man; 'he's just up from Bandra, and he's after them WG's that came here last winter; you remember my telling yer, don't yer?'

'Somebody did at the muster,' answered the girl in a careless way. 'Didn't Jem

Atkins say there were no calves or else Roper wouldn't leave them long. How do you do, Mr. Hall? So you haven't quite forgot the road over here? What do you think of this part of the country, Mr. Claythorpe?'

All this time I'd been looking at the girl with both my eyes, and wondering how she came to be what she was, and so different from any woman I'd ever seen. To begin with she was tall—taller than most women, slight made, but ever so handsome. She had large dark eyes and splendid teeth. Her voice had a wonderful soft low tone in it, and when she laughed it was pleasant to hear—like a child's. She spoke more like a lady I thought than a country girl. I was regularly thunder-struck.

'It's a very fine part of the country, I should say,' I stammered out. 'I never thought it was anything like this.'

'It's a fine place for grass,' she said 'in a wet season, but that's all that's good about it. I think it horribly dull, wet or dry; I'm glad to see even Jack Hall, if he only knew it. Mr. Roper's is a lovely place, I believe.'

'You're laughing at us now, Miss Barker,' says Jack rather sulky. 'You oughtn't to run down the country at any rate, or them that live in it.'

'Because I was born here, I suppose, Mr. Jack Hall. I don't see that at all. I'd have been born in Bathurst, or Sydney, or London if they'd asked me, but they didn't; and now I'll get you some tea; I've no doubt you're hungry enough, and thirsty too.'

She went out into another room—walked out like a young duchess. There was a strong good-sized table, big enough to dine a dozen people. A shy young girl of fourteen, dark like herself, brought in a clean table-cloth and afterwards everything that made up a real good tea-dinner; corned beef, boiled eggs, good bread, and capital milk and butter, with a big tin teapot full of strong tea.

When it was all ready, she called us in and sat in the room while we went to work at the eatables.

She talked away to Jack Hall most of the time, but found a way to ask me some questions about Bandra and Mr. and Mrs. Buffray. She supposed it was a grand place, and she'd always heard Mrs. Buffray was such a nice woman.

'So she was,' I said. 'Nobody could be kinder than she was to my sister Jane.'

'So you have a sister, then,' she said. 'Did she come out with you?'

'Yes, we had come out together.'

'And did she like this country? Didn't she hate it after England?'

'No; both of us liked this country better than England—intended to live in it all our lives.'

'How strange!' she said; 'I used to read such lovely things about England when I was at school. It made me cry when I thought I should never have a chance to see them all my life. Now I think this is a frightful country, with nothing to do but look after these tiresome sheep and cattle in good years, and to stand by and see them die in bad ones.'

'Still it's a good country to make money in,' I said.

'Perhaps it is. I don't care much about money. You see, people have to wait so long before they get any. What's the use of having money when you're old, like Mr. Burdock? Why his hair and his beard are the colour of THAT'—and she pointed to a calico bag, where the flour had just been emptied out, beside a door.

'People seem to be able to do without money sometimes here,' I said. 'That's where you have the best of it. But we can't get on without it in the old country.'

'I don't know how it is in towns,' she said, 'I've only been in Bathurst; but in the bush people only seem to think of two things—hard work and drinking. When they're not doing one, they're always at the other. I'd go away from the bush to-morrow if I could.'

'And have no more riding, Miss Possie?' said Jack Hall. 'No more gallops on Cooramen! Remember the ride we had across the Wild Horse Plain last winter, and the way you passed that new chum on the chestnut—like a flash of lightning.'

'That was pretty good fun, I dare say,' she says, and her eyes lit and flashed as if a fire blazed up inside of 'em, while she raised her head like a hound listening for the cry of the leading dog of the pack. She looked a handsome girl then, and no mistake. 'A good horse is worth having, and a real day's mustering is something like, when you haven't done anything or seen anybody for half a year, but it gets tiresome in the end.'

'We all have to do a lot of things we don't like,' says I. 'I never expected anything else before I came out here. Nobody has the right to go his own way in England—that is, unless he's a rich man.'

'Oh! I don't pity you men at all,' says she, with a toss of her head. 'You can go away when you like; and if you save your money, and don't spend it like fools, you're able to do pretty well anything you have a mind to.'

'There's a many people seem to like this part middlin' well,' says Jack Hall; 'they never go away anyhow. I've seen the same lot this years. They don't want no change, and if they did they haven't the money to pay for it.'

'That's where it is,' says she; 'they spend the money that might take them to some place worth seeing in bad grog at a dirty public-house. They haven't as much sense as my poor mother's people, that had the country before them. They never wanted any grog; they lived where God placed them; they hunted and fished from one side of their "tauri" to the other; and when their time came, died without fear or pain.'

'And quite right too,' says Jack. 'Now I think Wallanbah's a first-rate place; it's my "tauri," and I could live there for ever. Mr. Burdock's going to put me up a real tidy slab hut with four rooms at Little Lake, and then I'll be looking about——'

'You'd better be looking about the paddock rails if you want to find your horses in the morning,' said Miss Possie sharply, 'and I'd advise you to start off at once.'

We were up at daylight. I ran up the horses; and it was just as well we'd hobbled Jack Hall's horse, for he jumped the fence, hobbles and all, in the night, and made towards home. But Talgai ran his track and fetched him back; he hadn't got more than two or three miles.

'Ain't you comin' to lend us a hand Miss Possie?' says Jack. 'It'll give us all our work to keep the cattle on the camp and cut out them outlaws by ourselves.'

'Oh! I daresay!' says she, 'You're a very harmless crowd—you Wallanbah and Yugil boys. I wouldn't like to trust you with "clearskins" for all that. I've heard stories, I can tell you. Perhaps I'll come to-morrow, and bring Kitty, but our horses are all in the bush.'

Jack brightened up at this. 'Oh! I see. Well, I wouldn't ask you to ride anything but Cooramen—unless you'd like to take a turn out of Warbreccan here—he'd carry you like a bird. We'll take two days anyhow, and it's a chance if that'll finish it off.'

Barker had started on ahead with his boy Johnny and Talgai; he told Jack to come another way, and start all the cattle he saw, so that we'd meet on the main camp, where the most of our cattle would be likely to turn up. Miss Possie went into the house, when Jack started off at a hand gallop, and I after him.

We rode out to one of the run-boundaries,

then over to a creek, through a wilga scrub afterwards, cracking our whips and starting big mobs of cattle every now and then, which all headed one way, and went off as hard as they could split. Breaking cattle in to a camp's a fine thing. It's the good old-fashioned way of mustering, and there's nothing like it, to my fancy. By 12 o'clock or thereabouts we made the main camp, on a sandhill by a big water hole, and a fine jolly mob of cattle we found there.

Two thousand head if there was a beast! all in tiptop condition; cows, calves, bullocks, and steers, rolling fat, and fit for the butcher, the whole boiling. We had a smoke after we'd polished off the bit of bread and corned beef we'd brought with us, and then we rode in among the cattle.

'Plenty feller WG here, I believe,' says Talgai. 'You bin look out that one yaller bullock; red feller that one, blue cow—all about——, that one fat too, my word!'

'There's the biggest lot of your mob here, Mr. Claythorpe,' says Barker; 'I miss a few leading cattle though. They'll be out with the Pine Cowall mob. We'll get them to-morrow, if we've luck. The best thing we can do now is to cut out all we've got here and get them home to the yard to-night. It'll take all our time. If you don't mind keeping the cattle on the camp, Jack and I can cut them out; Talgai and my Johnny 'll mind them when they're drafted.'

We started to work. It took some galloping; but the ground was open, and the horses were in good buckle; the WG cattle had been driven all the way from Queensland, and after a flirt or two settled down as they were cut out with some station cattle to begin with.

We got away with them an hour before dark, letting the station cattle draw off the camp, of course; and though it was starlight by the time we got to Boree, we yarded 'em all right, and fastened the gates with a hide rope to make safe. Possie had no end of a tea for us. She'd dressed herself too, and had a bit of red ribbon and a silver cross on, that made poor Jack ready to go down on his knees and worship her.

CHAPTER VIII

COORAMEN AND THE WG'S

WE had a real pleasant evening, the best I'd had since I left Bandra. There was a piano in the big room that I hadn't noticed when we went in first, and Possie played, and sang too, 'like one o'clock,' as Jack Hall said. She *could* play. I'd never heard anybody like her. Of course I wasn't likely to. Miss Walsingham at the Hall in Applegate, I knew, played and sang, because I used to hear her through the door as I walked up and down the passage at odd times; and sister Jane said Mrs. Buffray had a sweet voice, and played all sorts of tunes, but I hadn't the chance to hear her close of course.

Now, here was this girl playing better than any one I'd ever heard in a music hall or in a theatre, and singing—by George!

Jack and I thought—like an angel. He sat with his mouth open and stared at her as if she was a new creature of some sort. He was ready to follow her about like a dog. Of course, like women do mostly, whatever colour they are, she didn't care a dump for him—ordered him about, and would hardly say a civil word to him. That's the way all the world over.

We'd had a deal of fun and nonsense that night. Possie said they'd got in the horses, and she was going to give us a hand on Cooramen next day. I was very glad of it. Then we went to bed.

'My word,' says Jack next morning, 'you'll see some riding as you may call riding to-day, when the cutting out begins; Cooramen was the best stock-horse on the Macquarie before they found out he was fast enough to win the Wilcannia Maiden Plate; the way he can walk round a bullock is something to look at.'

'All the credit belongs to the horse, Mr. Hall,' says she, mischievous like. 'The girl that steers him has nothing to do with it, I suppose?'

'You know better than that,' says poor Jack, 'but the old horse *is* a ripper and no mistake. You don't want me to blow about your ridin', I suppose. That'll tell for itself when we get to the camp. But there's no pleasin' you. The last time I told that young fellow from Coranga as you'd forgot more about riding than he ever learnt, you said it looked as if you couldn't do anything else.'

'Girls *are* hard to please sometimes, and that's the truth, Jack,' she says, and smiled at him in a way that nearly made him drop his knife and fork (it was at breakfast) to look at her. 'If you knew as much about them as you do about horses you'd be aware of the fact. But I'm going to be very good-tempered to-day and enjoy myself, so you've to look pleasant, and see that my saddle's well girthed and won't slip round.'

Jack was quite pacified by this, and came up with her horse directly after breakfast. Cooramen, as they called him, was a beauty without paint, sure enough. I wondered how they got such a horse in the family. However, it turned out that old George had backed him one day for a selling race at a bush meeting, and when he was put to auction, bid up for him like a man, and bought him over his owner's head. He knew the horse before, and he was that fond of Possie as he'd have done any mortal thing to please her, so he didn't grudge paying a bit high. Besides, what he'd won on him made him come cheaper, and there was an off chance as he'd pull off another race or two on the quiet before his legs went. He was a dark brown horse, about fifteen hands, but when he held up his head he looked half a hand higher. He had a drop of Arab blood in him, Jack said. They used to get 'em down from India in the old days. Anyhow, he was a regular plum, such as you see every now and then in all the colonies. Fast—game—wiry—with legs and feet like iron; up to weight, and good across country. You can't put 'em wrong with fair play. He's a lucky man that gets one or two of them in his lifetime, and my advice is always to stick to 'em, and never sell 'em while you've a shirt to your back.

Well, away we went. Possie had the old horse led up to the edge of the verandah and swung herself into the saddle as light as a bird. She had a nice side-saddle, and a regular stunning cloth habit, made by a tailor. It showed off her figure—one of the grandest ever a woman had. She had wonderful small hands—like a child's they were, and feet to match. When she walked she was that springy and graceful like she put me in mind of the tame doe there used to be in the Squire's park at Applegate. Her eyes were so dark and soft (when she liked) that they made her more and more like some shy, light-stepping wild creature, that seemed when she was startled as if she could jump over a house or fly into a tree. Sometimes, when Possie was walking up and down in a bit of a tantrum like, she put me more in mind of the tigress I saw in a cage at the Zoo, in London. But that was long after, and don't come into this part of my story.

Well, away we went, the whole boiling of us, for Back Boree that morning. It was a clear warm day, about an hour after sunrise. First of all old George went ahead with his boy Johnny, and his next girl Kitty alongside

K

of him. She was a slip of a girl about fourteen, with big eyes and a shy look, but full of fun and mischief underneath. She had a ragged gray tweed skirt on, an old straw hat, and she rode on a man's saddle with one stirrup over the pommel, and sat as straight and lissome as if she'd the best side-saddle in the world. She could ride anything, I believe, and her father said he'd sooner have her with him after wild cattle than any stockrider in the country. Both girls had stockwhips, made light, and with 'myall' handles (the native wood that smells like violets); before the day was over I saw that they knew how to use them.

Jack rode on one side of Possie and I on the other. Talgai came behind all by himself, but that didn't trouble him much; he wasn't over fond of company at the best of times. After we'd ridden seven or eight miles we came to a plain at the edge of a wilga scrub. Then the old man pulls up and lays out the different lines we're to take.

'You two girls come along o' me, I'm a goin' up to the Pine Cowall, and you're both on your best at the scrub racket. It'll take some galloping to wheel that poley brindle's mob, and if they once break there's no headin' 'em. Jack Hall, you can follow the creek up till you come to them sand-hills—there's one big mob run that way. You'd as well take Mr. Claythorpe with you. Johnny, you and Talgai sweep in all the plain cattle between here and the yellow water-hole, and don't you be larkin' or kangarooin', else I'll lay my stock-whip into you when we come to the camp.'

Johnny rode away rather solemn lookin', with Talgai after him; then the old man started off with the girls on each side of him, as if they were all entered for a three mile heat. Jack looked after 'em for a bit, rather grave like. 'Confound that old George,' he says, 'he might have left Possie with us; but I suppose he reckoned we might get lost. I expect there's some calves among them scrub cattle, and the old cove thinks it's a handy chance to get them. They'll be pretty smart cattle that gets away from Poss on Cooramen to-day; let alone Kitty.'

We'd all brought in our mobs by about two o'clock, and sat on our horses waiting for best part of an hour before we heard the roaring of George's mob coming closer and closer; by and by a faint crack of a whip now and again. There was a good-sized plain that came close up to the forest, and through this they had to come.

We all had our horses ready, for some of us were sitting side-ways on the saddle smoking and resting, when we saw a big brindled poley bullock dash into the plain, with a long string of cattle behind him, and make for the camp. They were coming pretty fast for fat cattle, as most of them were, and the brindled bullock and the dozen or two leading cattle had their tongues out. It was a heavy mob, five or six hundred at least. It took some time for the 'tail,' with all the slower quiet cattle and cows and calves to clear the forest. Last of all out they come, every beast, with Possie on the right side of 'em, Kitty in the middle, and George and his two dogs on the left flank. 'Little Kitty's had a buster or something,' says Jack, 'run against a tree, perhaps. She's got her bridle in her right hand and her whip's tied to her saddle.'

We rode up a bit nearer to the string of

cattle that were making into the main drove collected on the camp, and Jack Hall looked sharply at them as they passed before us. I couldn't make out—having seen so little of that kind of work—how it was that he could tell one beast from another in such a mixed-up mob, and so quick too.

'There's a snailey Wallanbah bullock I haven't seen this two years,' says he, 'and that sheeted red and white BL cow with the red heifer calf. She was a heifer when she got away from Wallanbah, and now she's a dashed fine cow, and, by George! there's that black bullock of ours, him with the wide horns. I thought he was dead. I never seen him so near a camp before. He always breaks when he sees the other cattle.'

'How's that? Is he like the crows and smells powder?'

'Can't say,' says Jack, 'but there's always a few cattle in every herd that's like that. They get cunning, and bolt back when they're near a yard or camp, for fear they'd be sent off, I expect. You'll see that joker'll bolt soon. Isn't he a slashing fine beast?'

The bullock Jack meant was a tremendous big beast, as fat as he could roll. On he came, with his head up, shaking his immense wide horns as if he was looking about him, and didn't know what he'd do next. All of a sudden he stops and wheels short to the right.

At that very moment we saw Cooramen give a plunge, and then go for him as hard as he could lay legs to the ground. The bullock was pretty near the lead, so that he had a fairish start. But the brown horse, now at top speed, overhauled the heavy beast stride by stride. 'Poss is going for him,' sings out Jack. 'Now you'll see some riding.'

It looked like it, as we both sat on our horses and watched the pair. I'd never seen anything like it before.

The bullock kept his own line, heading back, sulky and savage, towards that part of the cattle run where he was accustomed to feed. Poss, leaning forward, as if she was riding a race, kept on the outside of the line he was going, cracking her whip, like a pistol shot, every now and then. He didn't turn his head. Presently she came up with him, and keeping just clear of his horns, laid the whip into him back and forward, as neat as any one I ever seen. He shook his head, but wouldn't turn ; every now and then he made a short rush at the horse. Cooramen—she had him well in hand of course—would be out of his road like a shot, and before the bullock was well round again her whip would be playing on him, making the hair fly and drawing the blood like a bushel bag of mosquitos.

Blest if she didn't get close up on his shoulder once and rush her horse against him, so that she turned him in spite of himself towards the cattle. Then he'd stop and shake his head and face her. She'd play with him and get away when he rushed, and then go at him, flaking him right and left as he turned, and edge him off towards the other cattle. He was nearly done with running too, he was so fat, and last of all he began to get pretty slow, and show signs of giving in. She stuck to him back and edge till at last he turned tail and hit out for the camp, as if he'd settled in his mind to give her best. Then she raised a shout and followed him up, dropping the whip into him right and left till he fairly broke into a gallop and lumbered in among the cattle quite beat and exhausted.

I couldn't help looking at the girl as she came flying in among the cattle after him, leaning forward in her saddle, with her lissome figure swaying gracefully with every motion of her horse. Her hair had come down too, and hung over her shoulders in great shining coils.

'Hurrah for Possie!' shouts Jack Hall, as we rode up to her. 'Mr. Claythorpe didn't ever see a girl ride like that in the old country, I'll be bound?'

'I don't think I ever did, or anywhere else,' says I. 'I couldn't do it to save my life, though I can ride a little in my own way.'

'I'm afraid I look rather wild just now,' she said, smiling and hoisting up her hair in a great knot behind, while Cooramen stood as still as a trooper, with the reins on his neck. 'But I never like to be beat, and that same bullock has got away from us times without number.'

'Once we get him to Wallanbah we'll put him in "the round yard," [1] says Jack, 'so as he won't stray away from home no more. Mr. Burdock ought to give you a new bridle or a bonnet, Miss Possie, after your running him in so clever.'

'I can buy my own bonnets and bridles, thank you,' she says. 'I don't want any of Mr. Burdock's presents.'

'Now then,' says old George, coming up, 'if you want them WG's home to-night, the sooner we set to work cutting on 'em out the better. Poss! you and Jack Hall's got the two slippiest nags; you'd better cut out, and Mr. Claythorpe can help ye. Kitty and I'll keep camp, while Johnny and Talgai mind the cut-out cattle.'

'All right, governor,' says Jack, 'my horse wants work, he's too fresh. What's up with poor Kit. Has she hurt her arm?'

'Pony fell in a stump-hole and shook her a bit. She'll be all right to-morrow. Now there's four of your bullocks all in one bunch; get to work all and run out any clearskin-calves; I spotted a few.'

[1] The harness cask.

There wasn't much talking for the next two hours. Jack picked out the four WG's, and a few cows and calves, which we put together under a tree to make a start with. Then it was quick work, hammer and tongs. One minute I'd see Possie edging out a wild-looking steer, till she got him clear of the camp. He'd trot a few yards and then gallop for his life, then stop dead and wheel.

That instant you'd see Cooramen halt as dead as if his feet had been nailed to the ground, while Possie's whip would come swinging round, and the small end drop on to him as if it was going to cut him in two. He'd start on again, then try a dart to the left, and Cooramen would be galloping neck and neck with him as if they were running a race. And mind you, a fresh wildish beast can go like smoke for a hundred yards. Then a prop and a wheel, but wherever he turned Cooramen and the stinging rattling whip would be in front of him, cutting, cracking, and whistling across eyes and nose, tail and shoulders, as the case might be. Last of all he'd head for the cut-out cattle, and trot in among them with bellows to mend, regularly bowled-out, out-paced and out-generalled.

Then back to the camp full split. Beast after beast would be run out, Jack Hall bringing another out as she went in, and the other way on. I managed to get a few, but somehow I couldn't do it half as quick as either of those two—couldn't pick out the bullocks in the camp either as they did, almost without looking at them. They were all got out in time, besides the black bullock, with a few Wallanbah cattle and about twenty yearlings which belonged—so George said—to the Boree herd, and had never had a brand on their hides.

That night we were home latish, and it took some time to make the cattle safe in the yard. Then we had to unsaddle and turn out the horses. Possie and her sister went into the house at once, taking Johnny to help them. Half an hour, I expect it was, before Jack and I got things fixed right (we didn't want to find the cattle gone in the morning, you know) and made ourselves ready for tea.

They hadn't lost much time either, for

Possie had changed her dress and put a rose in her hair. The tea was all ready and waiting for us. There was no grog, of course. Men like George Barker never keep it in their house. They can't answer for themselves, so they don't have any at all. If they want a drink they go away from home, and as that don't happen above two or three times a year, it doesn't matter so much. I shouldn't have taken any if there had been gallons of it, and though Jack Hall liked it well, he could do without it for months at a time when he chose. Anyhow, we made a merry meal of it—no end of fun and chaff over the day's doings. Poor Kit's arm was found to be only bruised after all, and we agreed that we'd got the most of the WG cattle. There would be only twenty or thirty short, and those we could come for at the next muster.

'So you're going away in the morning,' Possie says. She'd been playing one or two pieces on the piano in a careless sort of way. She wouldn't sing—said she'd made herself hoarse.

'Yes. I must go back. It wouldn't be

worth while stopping another day and giving so much trouble for a few head. I'd come to next muster, whenever that was, if I could manage it.'

'Would I really?' That would be in October. There would be races afterwards at Calyanbone. She'd some notion of running Cooramen for the town plate and handicap, only there was no one she could trust him to—that is, that could ride the weight.

I'd make a point of coming over, I told her. I'd ride the horse willingly for her besides, if she could have him got fit.

Her face brightened up at this. She knew I was a first-class jock, she said. Somebody had told her about Tornado and the Juanbong Plate. It's wonderful how things travel in the bush. Anyhow, before I said goodnight I promised faithfully to come to the muster and ride Cooramen at the Wallanbah races.

She told Jack Hall, with great triumph, but he didn't seem to be so pleased as she expected. She thought it quite strange.

We cleared out next day for Wallanbah in

real good form. I was up early to see if the cattle were right and to make sure of Talgai getting the horses, when I found George Barker and his boy had just killed a fat calf. They were cutting veal chops and getting the sweet-bread for our breakfast. Fresh meat's always reckoned a treat in the bush. They drew up the hind quarters on the gallows where the bullocks were hung, but to my surprise cut off the fore quarters and gave them to the dogs.

'Isn't that wasting good meat?' I couldn't help saying.

'Not at all,' says George; 'we've often to kill a precious sight more heifers' calves than we can eat. We'll be tired of veal by the time we've finished the hind quarters of this one, and salt's too dear in this part of the country to waste it on a calf.'

Whatever would they say in Applegate? I thought to myself. There's half this fine body of veal, mud-fat, and tender as a chicken, worth a shilling a pound there; besides, what would some of the poor hungry families at home give for these ribs and shoulders? This is a plentiful country and no mistake ; there's enough and to spare, any child may see. It will go hard if Jesse Claythorpe don't save something for himself out of the land and the stock, and the money that's going begging here.

CHAPTER IX

JACK LEIGHTON, SWAGMAN

Possie and the boy Johnny came with us as far as the first plain, just to help us off the run. She kept quieter a deal this time than the day before, and looked as if she was out of sorts a bit. She spoke very little to either of us, but rode on ahead with the leading cattle, and as I was behind, and Jack on the other side looking out sharp in case any wanted to break, there wasn't much chance of a talk. Her brother Johnny and Talgai kept at the tail, and seemed to have all the fun of the party between 'em. I couldn't help looking at him and then at her. He was very near as dark as Talgai, with just the same kind of sleepy ways when he wasn't roused, while Possie and Kit were as fair as lots of English girls I've seen. There was nothing about 'em different from any other of the white natives—except that they were a deal better looking, and walked and held themselves better. Possie had wonderfully good teeth, as white as milk, and her dark eyes, that used to look so mournful sometimes, would brighten up when she smiled, so that you couldn't help thinking what a merry happy creature she was. She and Johnny said good-bye to us both, and went off back as soon as the cattle were steadied. She rode quiet for a hundred yards or so, and then set the old horse going, and was soon out of sight. I caught myself thinking about her for the next hour or two, and Jack Hall, I expect, was a good deal in the same line.

When we got to Wallanbah, Mr. Burdock was knocking about the yards and saw us come in. 'My word,' he says, 'you've got a fine lot of bullocks there, fattened on another man's grass. However, we must give and take. A few cattle's keep's neither here nor there, as long as we get country for ten pound a block, Crown rent.'

'How much is a block?'

L

'Five miles square,' he answers; 'of course there's water to be made, and there'll be fencing by and by; but it's a fairish grazing farm for the money, ain't it? Anyhow they'd call it one where I came from.'

'I should think it was,' says I, 'especially when it tops up cattle like that.' And there's no doubt a lot of these WG's were shaking fat. 'Is there any more land to be got at that price?'

'Plenty more, and cheaper too if you know the right way to go about it,' says he. 'Come inside and we'll have another yarn. I'm a-goin' over to Bynjewong to-morrow and I shan't see you for a bit. Oh! I forgot; what d'ye think of Possie Barker? Ain't she a stunner? There ain't many of these eddicated gals as hold their heads so high that's a patch on her, I think.'

'She's a clever girl,' says I, 'and good-looking too, there's no mistake about that; and I never saw a woman that could ride like her before.'

'You'll have Jack Hall goin' for ye if ye don't look out,' he says, laughing. 'And now we'd better come inside; my leg ain't quite right yet, and standing about tires me.'

After tea the old man mixed his brandy and water like he did before, and settled down for a solid yarn, as he said.

'I've been and taken a fancy to you, Claythorpe,' he says, by and by. 'I've good reason to owe you something for doing me a good turn that day on the plain. Still it ain't that altogether. I can see you're a young feller that's bound to get on in this country; that's got sense enough to keep a bit of money together, and not spend it foolish directly it comes. I'm not one of them chaps that'll entice a man away from his employer. Buffray's been a good friend to you, and of course you'll stay with him as long as he's got work to do. But I don't believe in Roper altogether, and so I tell you. Buffray gives him his own way a deal too much for my fancy. I told him that before Roper's face one day. He'll find him out yet. He ain't the man he takes him for, and before long you and he won't hit it. You ain't his sort, I can see. And when he tells you to clear—as he's most sure to do some day—there's a home for you at Wallanbah, wet season or dry, and a welcome too.'

We landed our cattle safe at Yugildah, and Roper seemed regular right down pleased for once that we'd got so many of the brand, and they looking so well.

'There's a man taking down fat cattle from Grambla,' says he, 'as will pass this way to-morrow. I'll draft the good ones out of the mob and send 'em down with him. Then there's no fear of them straying again. Mr. Blake won't mind obliging the boss, and I'll send a young chap with 'em. I'll tail the rest for a week or two, and turn 'em out with a quiet mob. How did ye get old Burdock to send Jack Hall with ye? Him and me ain't cousins, and I didn't expect he'd give ye a lift like that.'

So I told him about the buggy accident, and our going with him to Wallanbah, with a general notion of the muster at Boree.

'George Barker's a dry old stick, ain't he?' says he, 'and Possie's a good-looking gal enough. They say he's had her eddicated, taught the pianner, and all that. More fool he! I say. All those half-bred brats of his are sure to give him the slip as they get older. It's wasting money and time to teach 'em anything, in my way of thinking.'

'They seem smart enough,' I said, careless like, for I didn't mean to tell him more than I could help; 'I don't suppose all the teaching they'll get will hurt 'em.'

The cattle went away all right, and we settled down to the regular everyday station work, and pretty dull it was. After being away at the other places, Yugildah looked more dreary like and miserable than ever. Unless we were all hard at work, there was nothing to cheer up any one, or to take the least interest in.

It was a splendid run—large, and well watered, and out and out healthy—but no money had been spent upon it. There were no improvements of any sort, so at last I began to feel mopish for want of somebody to talk to, or something to do.

First of all Talgai and I got all the colts in and rode them, so as to keep them quiet. The most part of them were steady enough, but some were more trouble than they were at first. That took up a month or so. Then we had mustering, or going round the run every other day—lovely rides some of them used to be—coming in after dark, and then to cook your own supper when you got back. I felt ready to grumble at this, but I'd determined not to mind trifles in a new country; and I thought if any one had given us as much beef steak or corned beef in England as we could eat, with bread, tea, and sugar in proportion, what a trifle we should have thought the *cooking* of it was!

Talgai and I were out on the run a goodish way from home one day when we dropped in with a mob of cattle that hadn't been yarded for a year or more by the looks of them. They were wild and no mistake; it was some time before we could get them to round up. There were a good many unbranded calves among them belonging to the station, so we started to bring them home. We hadn't gone far before we came on another mob, camped. It was a bigger one than what we had with us. I stopped with the cattle, and sent Talgai over to look at them.

'Name that one,' I says, when he came back.

'All about cow and calf belonging to Thoresby,' says he. 'Calf not branded.'

'You see um Yugildah calf?' I said.

'No; like it four feller bullock. That one run here long time.'

'How far longa Mr. Thoresby's station?' I said.

'Mindorah five mile, close up.'

'You yan alonga head station, Talgai, and yabber that one calf alonga this one camp. Mine quambi alonga cattle.'

Talgai looked a bit astonished, but he always did what I told him. I'd broke him in to that. So off he sets. The cattle stopped quiet in the camp. It was pretty hot, so I pulled up under a tree and laid myself out to wait for an hour or two till he came back.

I hadn't been half an hour by myself when I heard horses, and back came Talgai with two men. Mr. Thoresby it was, and his stock-rider. It seems they were out too, and Talgai fell across their tracks accidental. The other cattle were within sight, and they rode up to them before they came over to me.

He was a square-built, jolly-looking, middle-aged man. His face was burnt a regular brick-dust red, but I was pretty sure he was an Englishman before he began to talk.

'Your name's Claythorpe,' he says, holding out his hand. 'Mine's Mark Thoresby, of Mindorah. You came up from Bandra to Yugildah with the horses : not long out from home. So you sent me word about these cows and calves here. Wonders'll never cease, will they, Ned?'

He and the stock-rider laughed as if it was a first-rate joke, and so did Talgai after a bit. I didn't see it, and said so.

'Oh! it's only our nonsense,' says he. 'I'm obliged to you all the same. If ever you're this near Mindorah again, mind you come over and see us. This chap knows the road,' pointing to Talgai. 'You tell Jim Roper you seen me, and I wanted to know if the Bishop had been at Yugildah and converted him like. He'll understand. You come over some day soon, or I'll think you don't want to be neighbourly.'

They went their way and we went ours. When I had put the cows and calves into the yard, I told Roper that we'd found a large lot of cattle with more calves, but that Talgai had said they were Mr. Thoresby's, and I had sent word to him to fetch them.

'*Sent word to him!*' says he, struck all of a heap. 'Why the h—l didn't ye bring 'em home to the yard with these others? How did ye know they was his? Weren't they on this run?'

'I believe they were half a mile over the boundary,' says I; 'but Talgai told me they were Mr. Thoresby's. He was quite certain.'

'Talgai be blowed!' says he; 'what's he know about brands. It's your business to bring all cattle as you find on this here run to Yugildah yard. When they're properly drafted they can be sent home, or they can come for 'em. But I don't believe in people taking cattle off this run without my seein' 'em.'

'What, not their own cattle?' says I. 'If they'd caught us driving those cows and calves they might have thought we were stealing them.'

'What the blazes business is it of yours,' says he, 'what they thought? What do *you* know about a cattle station, just off the ship? If you think you're to act boss here because you can ride a bit and had the luck to pull off a twenty-pound handicap, you've most infernally mistook your lay, and so I tell you.'

'I know I've not been long out of England, Mr. Roper,' says I, 'but I suppose the law about your own and other people's property is the same here as there. If you think I'm going to help you or any one else to steal cattle you've made a mistake, and a big one too.'

'I've two minds to kick you off the place,' says he, looking as mad as a wild bullock, 'and only the boss sent you here I'd do so, dashed quick. You come up to-morrow morning and I'll settle with ye, you can go back to Bandra then and tell the boss I sent ye.'

'You needn't try to bully me,' says I, looking him in the eye, 'if you'd like to get your hands on me, don't baulk your fancy. But I don't want a row for the sake of Mr.

Buffray. I shall go over to Wallanbah from here.'

'You may go to h——, for anything I care,' says he, and he turns his back and makes off home.

He was a bit cooler next morning, and seemed as if he'd like to make it up; but I'd had enough of Yugildah, and being sure we'd have another row if I stopped, thought it was best to clear when I'd got right on my side. He made out the time I'd been up and paid me at the rate of a pound a week. That was the regular wages on a station then. I'd only drawn some tobacco out of the store so I had a fairish cheque. For horse-breaking I ought to have had extra, but I didn't bother. I thought myself pretty well paid, and it hadn't all been hard work.

Talgai came up with me.

'You yan away, Mahmee?' he says, 'Talgai baal sit down alonga Yugildah; first time that one Roper bung (shoot) this one blackfellow, I b'leeve.'

'So you're a-going too, you black santipee, are ye?' says Roper, glaring at him; and if I hadn't been there I believe he'd a half killed the poor feller. 'The place is well rid of the pair of ye, in my opinion. I don't want no crawlers about Yugildah, only don't let me catch ye on the run after to-day, or by —— I'll shoot ye as soon as I would a dingo.'

We cleared next day, mighty glad both of us to be shut of Yugildah and Jim Roper. We had to stop on the road one night, and next day we reckoned to get to Wallanbah. We were going along a bush track that led into the main road to Wallanbah near the end of the day when we pulled up a swagman. He was walking very slow; he was a bit lame too. His swag wasn't heavy, for he had only a rag of a blue blanket, a billy of water in his hand, and very little else.

'Hot day, mate?' says he, as we came up.

'You're right there, how far are you going?'

'To Wallanbah,' says he, 'and that's a good ten miles by my reckoning. My feet are not up to much; I'm pretty well done up, and out of tobacco besides. Happen to have any about you?'

I pulled out half a fig of 'negrohead'; he took it as if he wanted it badly, and cut off an inch or so which he put in his mouth at once. As he did so I took a good look at him.

He was a slight, well-made, good-looking man, rather above the middle size, but not tall; brown hair and beard that just showed a few streaks of gray. His hands were burnt the same colour as his face, which was nearly black, and they were knotted and hardened with work, as any one might see. His shirt and trousers were worn and in holes; his boots were broken and pretty well done for— that was what made him lame. One of his feet had been bleeding, I could see from his 'toe-rag,' which stuck out on one side. A regular station hand he looked, on the 'wallaby track' as they call it, out of luck. His last shilling spent, tramping on without food, clothes, or a penny in the world, till he met with a fresh job of work. I'd seen dozens before like him, but somehow I kept looking at him, and looked and looked again.

'So you're going there too?' he said,

'that's a piece of luck; I've worked for old Sam Burdock before, and there's no better men's hut in the district. You tell him Jack Leighton's coming along, and he'll find me work of some sort. What are you on for?'

'I'm going to stop there for a week or two,' says I. 'I know Mr. Burdock a little, and he asked me.'

'You're not long out from home?' he said, looking pretty straight at me. 'English, I see. What county?'

'East Kent. I've only been here a year and a half—since I left Applegate.'

'By Jove!' said the swagman, 'you don't say so. This is a rum place to meet a man of Kent. Applegate—Applegate on the Stour—why, that's where I came from. What's your name, may I ask?'

'Claythorpe,' says I, looking at him again and wondering in my own mind how he knew about Applegate. 'And what did you say yours was?'

'So you're a son of Job Claythorpe, are you?' says he, looking hard at me. 'I used to play with your brother Dick—the one that was hurt in that poaching row. Poor Dick! Did you ever hear of the Leightons, of King's Leighton? I'm one of them.'

'Good God!' I said, 'you're never Reggie Leighton? My sister Jane used to tell me all about the day your people went to see you off when you were coming out to Australia. I was a little chap then, of course, and didn't know. Then you're Mr. Reginald? I thought there was something I knew about you. However did you lose your money and get down to this?'

'Down to this!' he says rather bitterly. 'You may well say that, Claythorpe; a broken-down swagman, without a shilling, and hardly a shoe to his foot! Well, bad luck, I suppose, bitter bad luck; most of it my own fault; that's the worst of it, you know.'

'I can lend you anything you want,' says I, eager enough. 'When we get to Mr. Burdock's he'll put you on to a job; I know I shall be there for a bit. You may trust me; you won't want anything that I can do for you. And now, you take my horse for a bit and we'll ride in turn. Squire

Leighton's son oughtn't to walk while Jesse Claythorpe rides, or else the world's coming to an end.'

The tears came into my eyes; I could hardly speak, it seemed so dreadful. I felt as if I could have stripped myself naked to clothe him in his poverty. I had never seen him that I knew of; but Mr. Reginald, Squire Leighton's son, from the grand old castle of a place, with its avenues three hundred years old, and its terraces and alleys, with the Dutch clipped yew and box trees, and the family chariot, and the eldest son that was in the Guards, I couldn't make myself believe that he was going to Burdock's men's hut, and glad to get there.

'It's Squire Leighton's son's own fault,' he says, frowning first and then smiling like; 'and if he has to walk it serves him dashed well right. You're a good fellow, Jesse, though; a man of Kent always stands up for his county. I'll take your horse for a mile or two, for this confounded foot of mine feels as if it were coming off.'

He took my horse; Talgai dismounted too and walked alongside of me. 'That one knock-about, big one tired,' says he, 'altogether that one lie down and quambi dead alonga road, I believe. Baal him, yan (get) along Wallanbah.'

There was plenty of time before us, and as long as we got to the station by sundown it didn't matter how easy we took it. We talked away about the old place until I felt quite a boy again.

He was the youngest son of Squire Leighton, and was a bit spoiled, and let have his own way after his brothers went out into the world. One was in the army, I knew, because we used to see him in his uniform when he came back at Christmas. He didn't always wear it, of course, but he had it on when there was a county ball, and at other times. The second was a clergyman, and had a parish not very far off. The third one was a lawyer in London, a book-learned man they said he was, and stood for the county once. This one was the fourth and youngest. He had my brother Dick with him shooting and fishing whenever he could. They were great friends as boys, and there's no doubt that Mr. Reginald would have taken him out to the colonies if he hadn't happened to get hurt just when he did.

This one was always inclined to be wild, and wouldn't take to his book. He could ride and shoot and fish with any man in the village when he was quite a little chap. The old Squire was very fond of him, and kept him at home long after he ought to have been at a public school like his brothers, people said. When he did go to school and college he did no good there, we heard in the village. Always up to some frolics, and spending a deal of money on racing and hunting. All manner of games he was up to, and at last he was sent home for a year, they said, and wasn't let go back.

Then it seems he took a wonderful fancy into his head to go out to Australia, and turn cattle and horse breeder. He'd been reading some book which said what a fine country it .was; that people did nothing but gallop about on horseback all day long, and so on. Anyhow, he wouldn't be said no to. So the old Squire at last gave him a couple of thousand pounds, and told him he'd send him three or four more when he was settled, and off he goes.

I just remember it being talked about as one of the wonders of the village when I was quite a little chap; everybody was astonished that the Squire could have the heart to let his son go to such a wild, far-away place. All his friends went to see him off; it was a nine days' wonder. After that it grew faint and forgotten, like Stephen Buffray's doing the same thing a lifetime ago. No doubt the Squire sent him the other thousands. No doubt there were letters at first, and crying over them by the sisters, and promises to come back in a year or two, when his fortune would be made. But the fortune was not made, somehow. The letters got fewer, then stopped altogether. The Squire died, and only the young ladies, his sisters, two of whom had never married, and lived in the old hall still, seemed to regret the handsome young man, full of hope and spirits, that had sailed away years ago for Botany Bay.

And here he was now, a ragged hard-up tramp, a 'knock-about,' as Talgai called him, not as well dressed as my black boy, and beholden to the son of one of his father's hinds for a lift on his journey, or a few shillings to carry him along.

How in the world was it possible for such a man to come to this? to sink so low? Clever, though not in the way of books, a gentleman born, belonging to one of the oldest families in England, manly too, full of work or fight when it was wanted; in a country where money was ten times as plentiful and easy got as in England; even supposing he'd lost all he brought with him by misfortunes or bad seasons, I couldn't make it out; whatever was the reason of it all?

If I'd been longer in the country I should have known what the reason was, the *only* one which ever knocks down a man worth calling a man in Australia, and *keeps him down*. Because he may fall once, then he's helped up always; twice—three times—perhaps even another time—if he's true to himself, by his friends. He's sure to have some if he's any good at all.

But I didn't know then for certain. I

thought perhaps he'd been very unfortunate, indeed, and it mightn't have been his fault altogether. I could see he'd worked and not played for years by the look of his hands, as were hard and horny, with the knuckles twisted, and the bones spread out and roughened,—besides being burnt as black as Talgai's nearly—working men's hands are all alike. There's no forging *that* certificate of manual labour. When I thought of what the Miss Leightons would have thought if they could have seen his hands at that minute, not to speak of the rough red folds of skin at the back of his neck, from years of exposure with nothing but a jersey or an old check shirt between him and the terrible sun, I thought I should have cried like a child. We were used to it, father and I, Tom and Dick, and all our lot from generation to generation. It was what we were born to go through—aboard ship or on land, it was all the same—we didn't expect anything better, and didn't grumble.

But there's something about gentlefolk and old blood—people may talk as they like —that stirs the heart of a true-born Englishman. When you think of what they're born to, the way they're brought up in a good county family, and you see one of them brought low in a strange land, it melts the very heart within you, and you feel as if you couldn't do enough for them.

These thoughts came into my head as we made our way along the dusty road. There hadn't been any rain for three months or so, and the weather was getting hotter and the country drier every day.

About a mile from the station we came to the Wallanbah Inn. It belonged to Mr. Burdock, who built it so that he mightn't be overrun with all sorts of travellers after he got married and had a family growing up. 'I was never to say stingy about a trifle of rations like "hungry Jackson,"' he said once, 'but having to feed perhaps from five to twenty strangers every night of your life is a little too much of the monkey, so I built this here hotel, which is a comfortable shop enough, and put Bill Bottrell into it, where they can have everything they like to call for, and pay for it if they've the money.'

We were passing the inn, when all of

a sudden Leighton said, 'Claythorpe, you haven't a note about you that you can lend me? If you have I'll borrow it to get a pair of boots from Bottrell's store; these things are so deuced disreputable, I don't like to face old Burdock in them.'

I pulled out a couple of pounds. I'd brought some cash with me in case I might want it.

'Better get a shirt or two, and anything else you want while you're about it,' says I. 'I'll leave Talgai's horse for you to ride up. We'll go on to the station.'

'All right,' he said. 'It's devilish kind of you. I'll not be ten minutes.'

He got off and hobbled into the bar, while Talgai and I went quietly up to the station.

'Mr. Burdock was out,' the servant said; 'but would be sure to be back for tea—say in half an hour.'

I put my horse in the paddock, and waited till nearly dark, expecting Leighton to come up every minute.

'You go alonga public-house, Talgai, look out that one mahmee, mundoee big one brokit.'

'I believe him wompi wompi alonga cobbra,' says Talgai, with a curious look in his eye, 'fust time me bring 'em Yarraman.'

So away goes Talgai along the road to the inn, and I walked into the verandah to wait till Mr. Burdock came.

CHAPTER X

MORE OF JACK LEIGHTON

I sat in a chair in the verandah thinking and thinking about Mr. Leighton. I couldn't get him out of my head. I hoped he would smarten himself up a bit, and then may be Burdock would ask him into the house, on my account, if I told him who he was. Fancy *me* being able to help a Leighton of King's Leighton, in that way. This *was* the other end of the world, and wrong side up, when it comes to that and no mistake. Perhaps we might go into partnership after a bit. I'd do the hard delving, and if we prospered, what a chance for him to go home to his people! and what an honour for me to bring it about! He'd soon get some of the tan off his face. Swell clothes do a lot, especially when a man's the real article underneath. I've seen them do a lot when he *wasn't*—for the matter of that. But his hands! They'd never come right, gloves or no gloves. They'd been knocked out of all shape and comeliness. I was real sorry about them, I can tell you. Just then I heard a heavy step and a loud voice, and in came old Burdock.

'Hulloo! so it's you?' he says, shaking hands as if my wrist was a hide rope that wanted stretching. 'So you've cut Yugildah? How's that; couldn't hit it off with Roper? I expected that—wonder you stood him as long as you did.'

'Yes,' I told him. 'I'd fell out with Roper.' I didn't say what for. 'He'd bullied me and I wouldn't stand it. That was all.'

Quite right too. What was I going to do? Going back to Bandra, after staying with him for a month?

'No; I was not going back. I had a great respect for Mr. Buffray; but there was nothing for me to do there that any weekly man couldn't manage. Of course if he wanted me, it was different. But I was going to strike out a new line for myself, if I could, or see a bit more of the country. Had a mind to go to Queensland.'

'That's the idea,' says he, rubbing his hands; 'there's nothing to be got by sticking about old settled districts like where Bandra is. A young man might as well stay in England, and so I've told a many of 'em. But tea's a-coming in. We'll have a yarn by and by.'

I told him about my sending Talgai to tell Thoresby about his calves. Then by degrees he picked out the story about Roper being wild with me for not bringing them home to the yard.

'Roper's two ends of a d—d scoundrel,' he bursts out; 'that's the long and short of it. He'll get straightened yet, smart as he thinks himself. I wonder Buffray keeps such a fellow about him, but he's had him this years, and he serves *him* well. Devil take him! It don't pay in the end though—cross work—and that he'll find. Did the black boy come with you. I thought I saw a darkie at Bottrell's. What's he doing there?'

'He went to see about his horse that I lent to a swagman we overtook. He was lame and done up. He was coming here to work, he said.'

'What's he want there then?' he says. 'What's his name?'

'Jack Leighton he called himself. He said you knew him; he comes from my part of the country.'

'Jack Leighton,' says he; 'of course I do; he ain't a bad feller to work, but the greatest swiper in the country. Of course you didn't lend him money. If you did you won't see him till it's gone.'

'It wasn't much. A couple of pounds,' says I. 'He wanted boots and a shirt or two. Does he drink hard then?'

Burdock laughed. 'You're not colonised yet. How the mischief *could* an eddicated chap like him get down that low unless he drank like a fish. *Why of course he drinks.* He'd sell his shirt for drink, and his soul after his shirt if any one would buy it these days.'

Here there was a knock at the door.

'Come in,' says Burdock, and in walks Talgai.

'Mine bin fetchum yarraman, Mahmee.'

'Where that one Massa,' I says.

'That one Bottrell put him alonga dead-house,' says Talgai.

'He's not dead! surely,' I said, regular stunned.

'Big one drinkum grog, that one massa, mine thinkit. All right one fella day. Me let go yarraman.'

'You let him go alonga paddock, Talgai,' says Burdock, 'and as it is pretty late, you get your supper in the kitchen here, yabba that our white Mary gib it tea. You yan men's hut by and by.'

'You'll know Jack another time,' he went on. 'You'd better have chucked that two pound into the creek. He'll turn up here some time to-morrow. Bottrell will give him a last nobbler and show him the door after breakfast. He ain't a bad chap when he's regular at work.'

'His name's not Jack at all,' I said right out, 'but Mr. Reginald Leighton, of King's Leighton, East Kent. They've been there since King Harold's time. He stopped there before the battle of Hastings.'

'He may be Lord Reginald, for all I know

or care either,' says the old man, filling his pipe again. 'He's been a sheep washer and knock-about man at Wallanbah these three or four shearings; been splitting or fencing and doing odd jobs in the slack time of the year. That's about all he's fit for now. He can earn his pound a week easy enough when he's at it, and generally has a middling good cheque to take after shearing; but he knocks it all down in one burst, and then has to hunt for a job like many another. Of course any one can know that he's been eddicated and seen better days. But once they take to the drink, that don't make a bit of difference. The well-bred 'uns are a turn worse than the others, it's my belief.'

'I should be so glad if you'd give him some work,' I said. 'I should like to try and get him to alter his ways.'

'You may try till you're black in the face,' says he, filling his glass; 'it won't do no good. Many a time I've thought I could help a man out of that ditch, but never saw one that didn't slip back. Work? of course I'll give him work. I've got some as wants doing, and when he's right no man can do it better. He'll be as well in a few days as ever he was. He'll tackle a six months' job, work like a horse, and never drink anything stronger than tea all the time. He'll get no grog, for he won't have any money—I'll see to that; and Bottrell dursn't give one of my hands grog on tick. He'll have boots out of the store, and good clothes, and borrow the newspaper regular. He'll be that clean and respectable-looking you won't hardly know him.'

'And what then?'

'What then? Why, I'll have to settle up with him some time or other, and he'll get his cheque—twenty pound or more. He won't spend it here. He'll go away, telling all the people he's going to Melbourne to take his passage for England to see his friends. That means he'll pull up at some pub about thirty or forty miles off, where he'll spend every shilling in a week, and then make off to another part of the country to begin over again.'

'What a dreadful thing,' says I; 'I can hardly bear to think of it. And you're sure there's no way of curing him of this—this—disease?'

'You may say that. It's the right name for it, Claythorpe,' the old chap answers, wiring into his second glass of grog. 'When it gets to that stage it's a real *disease*, just like scarlet fever or typhus. You might as well say to a chap with one of them things burning his life out, "What a fool you was to catch these 'ere; why don't you get well? You can, if you like, you know," and all that. Of course they can—if they're about ten men rolled into one, with ten men's strength. But being as they're made—only one at a time—with the work, and the climate, and the ways of the country being all agin 'em, and their own heart, why, they never do get well—and that's all about it. And now let's have a talk about something else. You'll see Jack to-morrow, and we'll find a box for him somewhere.'

There was no use, as he said, saying any more about the matter. Nothing could be done till next morning, when he would most likely come over. I hardly reckoned on it myself, but Burdock knew him better than I did.

'You come into this other room,' says the

old man, after a long smoke, 'and I'll show you something.'

So we went into a large half-furnished room, where there were two or three rough-looking tables, besides shelves with books and newspapers and *Government Gazettes*. I knew what these last were for; I'd seen Roper look over them for impounding notices, lists of brands, and things of that sort.

He lighted a lamp, and set it on one of the tables. Then he brings over a big map, and lays it on the table before us.

'Now you see what this is. It's a map with tracings of all the runs in this part, from the Survey Office, with their boundaries, roads, creeks, and all the rest, besides the outside blocks. There's a lot of them only part surveyed. There's the points of the compass. We're in the north-west division as they call it. Here's Wallanbah, you see, and Yugildah, and Mindorah, and Boree, and the whole lot of 'em. You can make that out easy, can't you?'

'Oh yes; that's plain enough.'

'Well—but look here. This isn't quite

so plain. Do you see that run they call Banya, next to another called Gol Gol. That boundary looks all right, don't it?'

'Yes, it does.'

'Well, it's all wrong. They don't join. The boundary's never been surveyed, and there's a bit of country in between, seven miles by five, or thereabouts, as they've no right to. Then there's those Yantara blocks—five of 'em—beyond. They're open for tender till the first of next month. There's a fortune starin' any man in the face, just where you're lookin'.'

'How do you make that out?'

'It's to be done this way. You or any one else can send in a tender for all unoccupied land between the boundaries of Banya and Gol Gol, Lower Warroo. D'ye see that?'

'Yes; but how am I to know that I should get it, or what could I do with it if I did?'

'You could do this as easy as falling off a log. You tender £12 : 10s. a year for each block. The others 'll most likely only tender £10 or £11. If your tender's accepted by the Lands Office, you can sell one or two of the blocks. They'll soon rise in value when it's known that somebody's got 'em. You make a start with a flock of sheep on one of 'em, then you can borrow a tidy bit of money from the banks " to make improvements with." '

'That seems a risk—to borrow money,' says I.

'You can't get on without some,' says he, 'unless you've got a goodish nest-egg. I'll put you up to the way they do it. But we'll go into it regular ship-shape to-morrow. You study over it a bit, and do as I tell you.'

Next morning we'd finished breakfast when we saw a man come through the outer gate. He carried a swag, and walked lame. It was Mr. Leighton safe enough.

'There comes Jack,' says the old man. 'I knew he'd turn up. He's got a head on him this morning, I'll be bound. But he's a plucky beggar; you couldn't kill him with an axe. There! he's stopped at the kitchen door. I'll go out to him. You'd better come too, and have it over.'

I didn't want to go, you may be sure. He would feel so ashamed at having degraded himself in my eyes, remembering what he had been and what I was. But I should meet him afterwards; perhaps it was best to have it over, as Burdock said.

He walked over when he saw us coming, loosened his swag from his shoulder, and put it on the ground. His face was pale and his eyes had a glazed appearance, but he held up his head and looked us both in the face. On his feet were the same identical broken boots—not a sign of anything new about him in the shape of clothes.

'Well, Jack, old man!' says Burdock, in a loud cheery voice. 'The old story, eh? Thought you was going to take to the blue ribbon this time. So you and Mr. Claythorpe's met afore, he tells me. Have you had your breakfast?'

'Well, no; I had a dip in the creek, and Bottrell gave me a pick-up, so I came straight away. Hang the place! If it hadn't been stuck right across the track, I should have come here all right.'

'Not you; you'd have found another shop, Jack, with them two notes in your pocket, if you'd had to swim the Murray for it. You'd better go into the kitchen and get your breakfast, and then toddle off to the men's hut, and lie down for a bit.'

'All right. I suppose you've got some work that you can put me on.'

'Any quantity. You can take a week's digging in the garden to begin with. Them weeds has been growing tremendious. And see here—come up at tea-time, and I'll give you a nobbler of "three star." It's the only one you'll get till you're settled with, so make much of it.'

'All right, sir,' he says. I heard him say *sir*, and it made me groan again. He said it as if he was used to it, too. After all, he was right. *They had changed places.* Burdock was the gentleman now—the squire, if you like—with his big house, his thousands in the bank, his freehold estates, his sheep and cattle and horses and carriage, fields and gardens, stables and coach-house.

All these things he had made and bought with his own shrewd brain and strong hands. This was the position of Samuel Burdock— once a shepherd—a ship's boy—a station hand. And Reginald Leighton, now called

'Jack,' whose youth was surrounded by luxury, was this man's labourer, a hewer of wood, a drawer of water, thankful to take his weekly wages, his beef and bread, a meal in his kitchen, a glass of brandy from his hand to ease the torments of the recovering drunkard.

'Here,' I thought to myself, 'is another Gurth; the thrall of a tyrant vice, and no smith may strike off *his* fetters.'

He stopped as he was going into the kitchen, and looked up at me with a bitter smile.

'A bad business, Claythorpe,' says he, 'but it's no use whining. You guess how it happened, I suppose; or Burdock told you. I can't resist the infernal grog, and that's the truth. It's been my ruin in this country, and will be the death of me yet. Your money will be all right. I will send you an order as soon as I've been here a month, and I'm likely to stop six.'

'Never mind the money,' I said hastily. 'If you only knew——'

'How sorry you are? I *do* know. I'm infernally sorry for myself sometimes. But the devil's too strong for me, and I have to give him best;' and now we'll drop the subject, if you please. I'm one of the hands on this place, and you're a friend of the boss. That's our position in the future, and we'd better keep to it. I feel as if a cup of tea would pick me up a bit. Good morning, Jesse, and thanks very much.' He walked into the kitchen, where breakfast was ready for him on the deal table.

Next morning early I saw him digging away in the garden as if he'd been brought up to it, whistling and seemingly quite well and jolly again. He went to the men's hut for his dinner, and came back again and dug till sundown—very quick and neat, too. It wasn't his first job of the kind, I could see. He said good morning or afternoon to me, as the case might be; but he didn't seem to care to talk much, so I didn't press it on him.

I couldn't help having another try with Burdock though. 'Don't you think if he could be got home to his friends that it might save him?'

'Not a bit of it. More likely to kill him in a year, besides disgracing them all. He's got the drink fever once and for all, and it won't never leave him as long as he's a living man.'

'But if he was out of the country?'

'Out of the country! That's the very thing that would be the death of him, quick. What can a swell that drinks do in England? Get into some disreputable hole and die there! He can't even turn billiard-marker. He can't dig or sheep-wash or plough *there*. Labour's dirt cheap, and the farmers don't want broken-down swells. But this is the best country in the world for him, and the like of him. He get's six months' honest well-paid work at a time, in the fresh bush air—well fed too, he is. It gives his constitution a chance to pull up. He ain't looked down on overmuch either, for people here understand his complaint, and *he* ain't the only one by a good many. The chances are he'll live longer, and do better "on the wallaby" here than in any other country in the world.'

'And be a "station hand"— a "knockabout man"—to the end of his miserable life,' says I.

'He ain't miserable, bless your heart!—far from it,' says Burdock. 'You can hear him whistling at his work now, as jolly as a sand-boy. They get used to it in time, and to the men's hut, somehow. They ain't comfortable nowhere else after carrying the swag for a year or two; and after their day's work, when they've had their supper and settled down to a good square smoke, they're as nigh happy as they know how to be.'

.   .   .   .   .   .

Burdock and I ciphered the thing out—as he called it—about the spare country between Banya and Gol Gol. The end of it was that I sent in tenders to the Lands Office for it, and the five Yantara blocks. He had printed forms and all that, and showed me how to fill them up, and send them off by post to the Department of Lands.

I was to stay there, of course, till I got an answer, and if the money came to more than I had in the bank, he'd advance me the rest. If I didn't get the block, I shouldn't want the money; and if I did, there was a 'gentle fortune' in it, as he said, which would be good security for a loan. Besides, there was a smart land agent in Sydney, who did all his work, that would push on matters at the Lands Office, and prevent their forgetting the case.

After a month or two's waiting, the paper came up from the Lands Office. My tender had been accepted for whatever unoccupied land lay between the boundaries of Banya and Gol Gol runs. A Government surveyor had been instructed to proceed to the locality and run the line; and the rent would be so much, besides the expense of survey, which I was directed to pay into the Treasury within three months.

Also—and this was a great matter—my tender for Yantara Blocks, A B C D and E, had been accepted, as per notice in the *Government Gazette* of —— date.

'You've made a dashed good start,' Burdock sings out when I showed him the letter, 'with your A B C blocks. There's nothin' to prevent your goin' in for the whole bloomin' alphabet by degrees. I knew them fellers at Wereboldra—that's the next station—would only tender £10 each. They didn't expect anybody knew about Yantara but themselves. They'll be ready to bite their fingers off when they see as you've got 'em. You're a made man, I consider. The next thing to see about is a flock or two of sheep. You can pick them up after Calyanbone Races.'

CHAPTER XI

MR. DORSETT, OF WESTBURN

AND now the race week was close on. The second week in December. The races were to be in the third week, so as to get them over comfortably before Christmas Day. Everybody keeps it a regular all-round holiday in Australia, just the same as they do in England. But what a difference there is in the climate. No snow—no cold wind—no wintry-looking trees. Everything warm—sunny—leaves on the trees and summer in the air.

Well, dust and hot winds aren't the nicest things going, but I'm blest if I don't think they're better for old people and poor people —for everybody—than the bitter days and terrible long nights of the old country.

Anyhow, people enjoy themselves in the

Christmas week in Australia if they never do at any other time. It's not too hot for fun and frolic, and to see the girls and boys skylarking about together, you'd think heat agreed with 'em, and that a hundred in the shade was quite the proper warmth.

Mr. Burdock and I were sitting at breakfast one morning when we saw, through the French window that opened on to the verandah, four horsemen coming along the plain. Riding at a walk they were, and making straight for the house.

'There's a police trooper with them. I see his boots,' says Burdock, whose far sight was as good as ever. 'The man on the off-side has got a horse like Roper's Quondong. You don't often see one walk like that. The trooper's horse has to jog to keep up with him. There's a black-boy behind, and a gentleman. He rides like one, anyhow.'

'There's something queer about Roper,' says I, 'if it *is* him. Yes, it's him, safe enough, and, by George! he's *handcuffed.* That's what's the matter. What in the world has he been up to?'

'We'll find out directly. I don't know the other man. He's a broad-shouldered chap, and looks deuced resolute. They're at the gate now. We'd as well go and meet 'em.'

They rode into the stable-yard as we got there. I could hardly believe my eyes. There was old Roper on his famous hackney, but the trooper had hold of the bridle-rein, and his rider's wrists were handcuffed together.

The gentleman behind rode forward, and I had a good look at him. He was a tall, well-built, very powerful man, I thought—with a stern and determined expression of countenance.

He spoke first: 'My name is Harrington Dorsett, and I am the manager of Westburn Station. You are Mr. Burdock, I believe, and a magistrate of the territory?'

'The same,' says Burdock, with a kind of a bow. 'What can I do for you?'

'I desire to bring this prisoner before you on a charge of cattle-stealing. I have my own evidence, and that of the trooper, that we found him in possession of cattle belonging to the Westburn Station, both branded and unbranded. I wish to apply for a remand warrant to the Bench at Wardell, where he can be further dealt with.'

'If you'll come into my office,' says Burdock, very solemn, 'I'll see what I can do. Mr. Roper, I'm dashed sorry to see you in this position—'pon my soul, I am.'

'It's all a mistake,' says Roper; but his lips seemed dry, and his voice sounded different from what it did generally. 'Mr. Dorsett's just come to this side of the country, and he don't understand the way we give and take here.'

'You'll understand *me* before I've done with you,' Mr. Dorsett says, between his teeth. 'Wando, hang up yarraman—man 'em this one, two fellow!'

The trooper got down first and helped Roper to alight. It ain't so easy to get down with no bridle to hold on by. I've watched prisoners trying to do it—active chaps, too—and they couldn't manage it well. Then he took him by the arm and followed Burdock into the little room in the verandah. The boss sat down with a book before him at the table, and the case began.

First the trooper gave his evidence.

'My name is James Brent, police mounted constable, stationed at Cobran. On the night of the 12th instant, from information received, I proceeded to Yugildah station, which I reached before daylight. I camped near the stock-yard in company with Mr. Dorsett, now present. I have reason to believe that he is the manager of Westburn Station. The aboriginal tracker, Wando, now present, had accompanied me from the police barracks. We remained behind a brush fence; we had put our horses into a disused hut, and fastened the door. Just before sunrise I saw two men come from the prisoner's house to the stock-yard. There were about a hundred head of cattle, I should say, chiefly cows and calves, in the stock-yard. The men made a fire, and having drafted off the calves, some of which were large, commenced to brand them. When they had finished, we walked down to the yard.

'Mr. Dorsett said to prisoner; "What do you mean by branding my calves, you infernal scoundrel?"

'Prisoner seemed taken aback and said:

"These were some cattle that had got mixed up with an outlying mob which belonged to the Yugildah herd. He would give calf for calf, as had been the custom with the station before."

'"You lie," says Mr. Dorsett. "These cows and calves have been tracked every foot of the way from our Sandy Camp. It's not the first haul you've had of the Westburn cattle. But I've caught you red-handed now, and by —— you shall suffer for it! Constable, inspect the brands of these cattle, and make a note of them."

'I did so accordingly. I counted fifty-four cows in the big yard, seven steers, and five heifers. They were all branded WWD.

'In the small yard, which was used as a branding pen, I counted forty-eight calves, from two months to twelve. They were fresh branded with the Yugildah station brand, BY, except ten of the best heifer calves, which were branded JR over 2—which I believe to be prisoner's private brand. When the calves were turned into the yard with the grown cattle, most of them began to suck the cows with the WWD brand.'

'Did the—did Mr. Roper say anything when you drafted 'em?' says Burdock.

'No—unless "it was all a mistake." He kept on saying that.'

'What was done then?'

'Mr. Dorsett—he says: "I give this man in charge for cattle-stealing. I am prepared to give evidence before the nearest magistrate."

'I arrested prisoner, and charged him with stealing certain calves, the property of the Messrs. Drummond, of Westburn Station, He answered that he had no intention of stealing them. I then conveyed him before the nearest magistrate.'

If we had waited till Mr. Burdock took all this down we should have waited a long time. He asked me at the first if I'd mind doing it; and as I could write a good plain hand, and had improved a bit keeping the station's accounts, I set to work and did it.

'You read it out, Mr. Claythorpe,' says Burdock, as solemn as a judge, and I did.

'James Roper,' says he, more solemn still, 'have you any questions to put to this witness?'

'Yes I have,' says Roper. 'When you put them cattle together, will you swear as the calves belonged to the cows in the big yard?'

'Well; I didn't ask 'em,' says the trooper; 'but I saw three-fourths of the calves start sucking the cows, which looked very like it.'

'Did I offer to prevent Mr. Dorsett and you from going through the cattle?'

'No; and it wouldn't have been much use if you had.'

'Are them cattle in my yard now?'

'No. Two of the Westburn stock-riders came up before we left and took them off home.'

'Did I offer to resist you in any way?'

'You made a boggle about being handcuffed, but when Mr. Dorsett put his revolver to your head, you gave in.'

'That will do,' says Roper. 'I see it's no use me asking any more questions.'

All this was taken down. It's a curious thing people in trouble always want to ask questions, and very seldom do themselves any good by it.

Then Mr. Dorsett was sworn, and gave his evidence.

'My name is Harrington Dorsett, and I am the manager of the Westburn Station. On the morning of the 12th instant I was at the Sandy Camp on the said run, in company with the aboriginal Wando now before the Bench. A large number of cattle were on the Camp. They appeared excited, as if recently disturbed. There had been rain in the night, and the ground was moist. My attention was directed by the aboriginal to some tracks of cattle leading in the direction of Yugildah Station. They appeared to have been going very fast or to have been driven. The aboriginal—by name Wando—then said: "That one likit cow and calf—all about! Yan along Yugildah, I believe."

'"You look out yarraman" (horses), I said.

'"Me seeum two feller track, Mahmee," he made answer. "This one likit belonger to Roper Quondong—fore foot turn in likit parrot."

'As it appeared that station cattle had been driven in the direction of Yugildah, I despatched the stock-rider to the police station for the last witness. He was then to return and bring another man to Yugildah. With the aid of the black-boy, I followed the tracks to Yugildah, a distance of fifteen miles, and found that a mob of cattle (including forty to fifty unbranded calves) had just been yarded. It was then dusk. I concealed myself until next morning, when the last witness arrived. I fully corroborate his statement as to the branding of the calves by prisoner. I gave him in charge for cattle-stealing. I now pray that the prisoner be remanded on warrant to the Court of Petty Sessions at Wardell, when further evidence will be forthcoming.'

'All right,' says Mr. Burdock, and then appearing to recollect himself, he frowned, and began to read and turn over the leaves of a big book which I afterwards found was Judge Wilkinson's *Australian Magistrate*.

Then he begins: 'Prisoner at the bar, have you anything to say for yourself. Anything you say will be taken down in writing——'

'That ain't it, your worship,' says the trooper, who was a smart young fellow and used to act as Acting Clerk of Petty Sessions at the small township he was stationed at. 'It's not a committal yet.'

'Oh!' says Mr. Burdock, 'here it is. You stand committed—no! I mean remanded to the Bench of Magistrates at Wardell for this day week, there to stand your trial—no, that's not it!—when fresh evidence will be brought agin you, and the Lord have mercy upon—no, that's not it! I mean, bail will not be allowed on no account. Constable, you'll find all the forms in that pigeon-hole. If you fish out a remand warrant and fill it up, I'll sign it. This Court stands adjourned till next time. You and Roper had better go into the kitchen and get a jolly good feed; you'll both want one before you get to Curbin. Mr. Dorsett, sir, perhaps you'll come inside and take some refreshment, as you've been a-campin' out all night, it seems.'

CHAPTER XII

THE FATAL LEAP

THEY waited an hour and fed their horses as well as themselves. They all looked tucked up, what with hard riding and camping out with nothing to eat. Then they went off—Mr. Dorsett and his boy one way, Constable Brent and Roper the other. I couldn't help feeling sorry for Roper, though he'd never showed himself a friend to me, when I saw him led away with the bracelets on him. The trooper made him change horses too, which, I expect, he felt worst of all. 'Quondong's too smart for this old screw of mine,' he says. 'You might fancy to make a bolt of it, and I couldn't see the way you went on him. You might, and you might not. Anyhow, I'll make safe. You take Dandaloo here; he ain't rough, and he know's he's going home.'

When he saw the trooper mount Quondong he gave one look as if he'd never realised the thing properly before. The old horse didn't like it either, for he snorted, and seemed half-minded to play up. I don't suppose he'd had a stranger on his back for years. But Brent gave him a chuck with the bit and a dig with the spurs that showed he was going to stand no nonsense, and away they went, Roper hangin' down his head and lookin' regular broke up.

'I must have a nip after that,' says Burdock. 'I feel quite down in the mouth, though it serves Jim Roper dashed well right. Here's a chap that's well off, saved money and got it in the bank, ain't married, and got neither chick nor child, and he goes and puts his head in a noose for the value of a few calves! But it ain't the first time. Many a clearskin he's nobbled afore now from Westburn, and many a fat beast went down with Buffray's cattle as *he* never knowed about.'

'What sentence will he get,' says I, 'if he's found guilty? They won't hang him, will they?'

'They used to do,' says Burdock, with a queer twist of his face; 'likewise for sheep-stealing, but that's past and gone. It was a trifle too hard when you come to think of it. But he'll get three years' imprisonment certain—perhaps five—depends upon the judge partly. He won't see Yugildah this Christmas, or the next either.'

. . . . . .

The first day of the great Calyanbone Race Meeting came at last. I'd nearly got tired of waiting, but up got the sun as usual somewhere about half-past four. Not a cloud in the sky—looking as if it wouldn't rain for a year. It hadn't been a bad season, so we didn't mind a spell of dry weather.

I'd been over pretty often to see Cooramen, or Possie—one of the two—and came back with a good notion of the horse and a soft feeling about the girl. He was in first rate trim—fit to run for a man's life, and I was regularly 'gone,' there was no mistake about that. I was going to ride Cooramen for the Town Plate and the Handicap. Whether I won or lost, I was going to ask Possie to be my wife the day after, and marry her if she said 'yes' as soon as I had a place to take her to. I'd thought it all over—for and against—a good many times. I knew that Jane wouldn't like it, and that things might be said about her colour, and all the rest. But no one could say a word against herself—that was the great thing. She was a good girl—a clever girl, and a handsome one, too—if ever there was one. When I thought of going away and leaving her, it seemed as if the thought would drag my heart up by the roots. If she said 'yes,' that settled it. It was my fate, as the gipsies say, and I wouldn't have given her up, if every man, woman, and child in Applegate had asked me to.

Calyanbone was five-and-twenty miles from Wallanbah. Burdock and I started with his buggy and pair of grays about eight o'clock, after an early breakfast, and were there quiet and comfortable before eleven. My word! the town was full. There were a lot of big squatting stations lying to the west and nor'-west of it, where they had improvements going on. Every man-Jack of the dam-sinkers, fencers, and station hands had come in. All the young gentlemen that were on the 'colonial experience' lay were there. They didn't often get such a chance. Only a few of the squatters themselves were in; most of them were in town, or at the seaside—and quite right, too. All the supers and under-overseers had come. If there'd been anything to steal from the stations except sheep, now would have been the time, for there was hardly a soul at home to look after anything.

We drove up to the best hotel, where Burdock had engaged rooms a month ago, or there'd have been very little chance of getting any. I was pretty well turned out—I'd learned to dress myself like the young fellows—and wasn't a bad-looking chap, though I say it, you boys! Not much for height, but neat made, and wiry. I was stronger than I looked, and as active as a cat. I hadn't a bad face—as faces go—fair hair and blue-gray eyes, goodish teeth and a firm-set mouth. I'd learned early to hold my tongue and say 'no'—a deuced good habit, and I kept it up; it's proved lucky for me many a time. Everybody seemed to know Burdock and shook hands with him, and he always introduced me as his friend, Mr. Claythorpe.

It's a curious thing — and I've often studied over it—how one man is made much of, and spoken of everywhere as Mr. So-and-so, while another never gets beyond Jack or Bill—or Smith or Jones—as the case may be. One man rises, and goes from high to higher; another gets lower day by day.

Newly-come people don't understand this. Generally they think that money does everything, and that there are no ranks or differences in colonial society.

There they're quite wrong. There are reasons and rules which help one man to get up, and keep another down, and their families, if they have any, with them. But newly-imported people are seldom sharp enough to see these causes till they've got the 'run of the ropes.'

It's partly this way. If a man gets a start in any position of trust or independence—if he has reasonable manners and self-respect—he has a good chance of getting into the 'reserved seats.' The bachelor squatters will take him up first; then some of the others, like Burdock, who are not very particular, having risen themselves. Afterwards people get accustomed to him, and he takes rank with the rest—that is *if he behaves* himself. If he doesn't, he gets shown the door and is shunted. A man who does labouring work, like Leighton, isn't let in, though he may be known to be a gentleman. People say there *must* be something wrong about him, which there is generally. He gets coarse in his ways too, and *always* drinks. I never knew one that didn't anyhow. Of course a steady young fellow might be unlucky. A little work wouldn't count against him then—rather be in his favour. But he must come out of it. If he doesn't, it shows that he deserves to stop there, and he is rated according.

So I found myself ticketed as 'a friend of old Burdock's, of Wallanbah, you know; not long from England. I had taken up those Yantara blocks; was a first-class amateur jock, and was going to ride for the Town Plate and Handicap.'

This was all the information that was wanted. I found myself quite popular, and was asked to 'take something' by dozens of young fellows, which I, of course, had to refuse.

Just before twelve o'clock I heard one of these young fellows say, 'By Jove! Charlie, what a handsome girl! Who is she?'

I looked, and there, sure enough, came Possie, riding the chestnut mare Giráh, wonderful well turned out, with her habit and hat, gloves and silver-mounted riding whip. The mare was in splendid buckle; her golden-coloured skin shone again, and though she reared once and plunged a bit when a horse passed her, she only showed off Possie's seat and hands by her tricks. Old George Barker was quite spruce, and Kitty rode close by him on the other side, looking half afraid of the crowd and the company.

'Johnny and Jack Hall came over with Cooramen last night,' she said, after we had shaken hands. 'They got a box for him, and won't show till he's saddled.'

'You'll come and lunch with us, Possie,' says Mr. Burdock, who'd come up behind us. 'Barker, you come too. There'll be some champagne going, I daresay.'

George 'wasn't sure. He might, and he mightn't. Possie would come, and Kit—much obliged to Mr. Burdock.'

I borrowed a horse and rode round the course with Possie, who seemed to be quite at home. She made me tell her everybody's name. I was amused to see how everybody almost turned and looked at her.

'They can't find any fault with my horse or my habit, that's one thing,' she said laughing. 'Giráh's rash and hot-tempered like her mistress, but she can behave herself when she likes. Why, there's Nellie Thoresby, of all people. I didn't know she'd returned from Sydney.'

As the words came out of her mouth I noticed her face change. It lost its happy child's look and a half frown came instead.

'Who is Nellie Thoresby, I've never seen her?' I said. Then I recollected that Thoresby had said something about 'his girl being away in Sydney.'

Just then a party of young men, with two or three of the country girls, on horseback, rode towards us, when one of them, a good-looking girl enough but no beauty (as I thought then), rode forward.

'Why, Possie dear, I haven't seen you for ages,' she said. 'Didn't you hear I'd come home? I expected you over a fortnight ago.'

'But I didn't know you had returned,' said Possie, in rather a stately way. 'If you told any one to tell me, they forgot all about it, thinking of you, I suppose. But I must introduce Mr. Claythorpe — this is Miss Thoresby, of Mindorah. I expect you have both heard of each other, haven't you now?' And she looked from one to the other as if she could read our hearts.

The other girl smiled. 'I certainly *have* heard about Mr. Claythorpe more than once. Father seemed to think it so good of him to send us word about those calves. He couldn't get it out of his head.'

'I don't wonder,' says Possie, 'such a thing was never done before at Yugildah, and never will be again most likely. But I didn't come here to talk about calves. I must go and have a last look at Cooramen.'

She gave the mare an impatient tap with

her whip as she said this, hit her harder than she thought perhaps, for Giráh made one jump, going up into the air with all four legs at once, and then gave a straight plunge as she went away which would have shifted most people. But Possie only swayed back in her saddle and let her go her best pace for a hundred yards, and then pulled her up with the greatest ease.

'Poor old pet, did it get a slap,' she said, 'from its naughty mistress. Never mind, she shall have sugar plums by and by,' and she stroked her mare's glossy neck, leaning forward like a child stooping for a flower. 'Now let us go and see Cooramen. When does our race start?'

'Three o'clock—just after lunch—so we shall have plenty of time to see everything and everybody.'

'That will be very nice,' she said.

'Somebody says something in a book about living an hour in a moment,' she said, turning suddenly to me. 'It is quite true. Do you know I feel so excited I can hardly sit in my saddle. It is such a wonderful change from the terrible sameness of our everyday life. I wonder if I shall be doomed to it for evermore.'

'Who knows?' I said. 'I am going to be your neighbour, you know. It is only fifty miles to Yantara; I shall always stop at your place coming in. I have got to make the station first—build huts, yards, paddocks, everything. I wish I was at it now.'

'That's not over-polite, is it?' she said laughing, 'but I know what you mean. You are quite right. I so often wish I was a man. But I would not be contented to do what they do. Why don't they work hard for years, spend nothing, and then go away to the beautiful other countries we hear and read of, and enjoy life. *This* is not life.'

'Just now you said it pleased you.'

'From the change only. Think what the other must be, when this appears a sort of heavenly vision to me. Well, I *think* you have a different notion of happiness. But here is dear old Cooramen. Doesn't he look a *king*?'

Jack Hall was leaning against the door of the loose box, smoking, as we rode up.

Johnny Barker was just drawing the sheets back over the old horse's shining back and quarters.

He was standing with the muzzle on in the roomy loose box, first lifting up one leg and then another, as if he was rather tired of doing nothing and wished the fun to begin.

Jack looked first at one and then the other of us. Then he said to Possie: 'I hope you're satisfied now,' and he showed his white teeth in a smile that was more than half good-humoured, though I knew he was vexed.

'Why should I be satisfied?' she said haughtily. 'And what business is it of yours?'

'Not much, of course,' he said, looking at her as a man looks at a child that he hasn't the heart to scold—'only you're well off to-day. You've got one man to look after your horse, and another to ride about the course with you, and both on the chance of pleasing you, I suppose. You'll want another while the race is being ridden. You could pick up one at lunch, if you tried.'

She turned her head a little, and looked at him for a moment. A spot of colour came on each cheek. Her eyes flashed again, and her lips parted for a moment before she spoke.

'Say another word like that, Jack Hall,' she answered, 'and I'll never speak to you again as long as I live. Who are you, to tell me what I'm to do and not to do? I can saddle Cooramen myself if you're tired of doing what you promised to do. Only say the word.'

She looked so handsome as she said this, not raising her voice, like another woman would have done, but putting a deep low tone into every word that had double the effect. The same feeling, I'm sure, was in both our hearts. We could not help admiring such a pretty creature, though she half frightened us. Like all men, though, we thought we could quieten the temper if we owned the owner of it.

Jack looked savage for a moment. Then he laughed. 'You'll start the old horse capering and make him lose the race, if you don't mind. You can blow me up sky-high when it's all over, but keep cool, for Cooramen's sake, till after the start.'

She raised her whip, half in anger, half in play, and then turned away. It was some time before she recovered herself and said: 'How provoking men are, and how foolish it is to lose one's temper. I wonder if I shall ever have mine under control. What leaps are those? They are stiff, are they not?'

'The steeple-chase jumps,' I said, 'to be run to-morrow. The stewards have had them made strong on purpose. They are safer that way, they think. The men won't try to gallop over them.'

'What's that one that seems higher than the others?'

'It is four feet six, good measure,' I said. 'A big jump.'

'I believe Giráh could do it,' she said, riding over and reining up the mare's head till she put her nose on the stout rail. 'I rode her over our paddock fence last week, and she flew it like a bird. It is quite as high, though I don't think it is as stiff.'

'Giráh can jump well enough,' I said, 'but

she is too hot to be safe. She takes her fences flying too, and some day will take off too near or too far off, and come down a smash.'

'Not she—will you, old lady?' she said, stroking the mare's neck. 'She knows my hand, and though she *will* race at her leaps, she picks herself up just at the right moment. I wish there was a jumping prize for us girls to-day, as they had at Bathurst.'

'I am very glad there is nothing of the sort,' I said. 'I'm always afraid of an accident happening.'

'That bay horse of Nellie Thoresby's can jump a little, they say. I should like to see her follow me and Giráh over these leaps.'

'What does it matter whether her horse can jump or not?' I said. 'She can't ride as well, though she hasn't a bad seat, I'll say that for her. I never saw the woman yet that could hold a candle to you in that line.'

'I like to hear you say so,' she said, looking at me as if she'd suddenly changed into another woman. 'All the same I should like to ride against her for once in a way.'

After the small events came off we had a first-rate lunch at Mr. Burdock's buggy. He'd got a case of champagne, and invited all the people he knew, the young swells and others, to take pot-luck, as he called it. We'd brought a famous big basket in the buggy with us, and had kept the old woman cutting sandwiches for I don't know how long the day before. There was a cold turkey and chickens, a capital ham, and, as I said before, plenty of champagne.

Everybody laughed and talked; Possie looked her best and came in for plenty of attention. I was surprised to see how cool and easy she took it, holding her own well, as if she'd been used to these kind of people all her life.

'What a nice mare that is of yours, Miss Barker,' said one of the back-block youngsters. 'Somebody said she would jump any fence on the course.'

'She is hard to beat over timber,' says Possie, quite composed like. 'I think she could take anything here.'

'That bay horse, Wallaroo, of Nellie Thoresby's, can jump well, too,' said another young fellow. 'Weston said she could win the steeple-chase, he knew, if she entered for it.'

'Not if Giráh was in it,' said Possie. 'I'd back her against the bay for all I'm worth in the world.'

'Suppose we had a trial for a new side-saddle and bridle,' said the first man who had spoken. 'Not a race, but a hunter's trial, after the handicap. It would be most interesting. What do you say, Miss Barker?'

'I'm ready if Nellie will ride,' says she. 'I'm not sure that her mother will let her, but you may try.'

'It's a splendid idea,' says the first man, whose name was Charleston. 'I'd give all the world to see it. I back Miss Barker here of course.'

'The jumps are high, and stiff too. It's a little dangerous,' I said. 'Perhaps some of you gentlemen will ride over them first.'

'I don't mind putting my old horse over after his race is run,' says Charleston. 'But we'll see about it by and by. Isn't time nearly up?'

We all went down to see Cooramen saddled. I had my jacket on underneath a light silk coat, so there was no dressing wanted. The old horse came out looking fit to run for the Melbourne Cup, and when I got a leg-up and felt him move away something like spring steel and velvet mixed, I knew he was bound to win.

'If he don't win to-day he'll never win,' says Jack Hall. 'You're carrying all the big money from here to the Macquarie, Mr. Claythorpe, so do your best. I'll cut the turf if you throw me over.'

'What one man can I'll do to-day, Jack,' I said. 'If there isn't a dark horse and Cooramen stands up we must win.'

. . . . .

It was a good race and a better finish, though I say it. The first favourite was a black horse, long and low set, with four white legs, Dolo by name. I was afraid of him from the first. He was queer on the near fore leg, but he'd run well in good company and had a name as a stayer. A professional had come up to ride him, and he was backed by most of the squatters round about, and the few bookmakers that had found their way up. There was a very fast gray mare known to be a good one, I doubted whether she could carry the weight; her name was Modesty. There was five others altogether, all pretty fair goers, but it was generally supposed the race lay between one of us three. Dolo came out of the stable of a big squatter who had half-a-dozen stations northward of Calyanbone. All the colonial experience young gentlemen and most of the working hands from the station, who'd got away to the race for a holiday, put all the money they could afford on him.

The saddling bell rang, and I walked quietly down to the stand, opposite which we were to start. Jack Hall led him and Possie rode a little way off inside of the ropes, looking at the old horse as he moved along, arching his neck, and playing with his bit, every inch a race-horse. I didn't think there were so many people on the course before. The two or three four-in-hand drags were crowded, and all the excitement of the crowd seemed to have been kept bottled up for this race.

I was fit, and the horse was fit. 'They shall have a run for their money,' I said to myself.

We got off to a middling good start. I sailed away a bit on the outside, and let the youngsters make the running. I never felt a horse go better under me than Cooramen did that morning. I steadied him, and only kept my place, knowing some of the leaders would come back to me before long; and they did. I drew up a bit as we passed into the straight opposite the stand, and couldn't find that he had half extended himself as yet.

The gray mare shot into the lead here, followed by the black horse, Dolo, the rider going pretty patient like myself, but beginning to waken up. The mare began to stretch away from us at such a rate of speed that we had to begin to ride not to be left behind. Just then a bright chestnut horse with a blaze down his face came up through the ruck on the inside, and challenged the gray mare. We let them go at each other, keeping well up, and of course reserving our final effort till we passed the turn.

The chestnut and the mare had a desperate rally, which ended in the horse drawing ahead. When we were about three parts of the way round for the second time, I set Cooramen going, and we four went at it. Dolo was a lazy horse, and his jock gave him the whip, which made him shoot ahead as if the others had been standing still. He passed the gray mare, then the chestnut, and the mob began to yell 'Dolo; Dolo wins,' and so on. I kept creeping up, doing all I knew, but not lifting the whip. I sat quiet, and let the old horse have his own way till the last fifty yards. Then I made the rush I had practised many a time before. I let him have whip and spurs both. Dolo's rider made a rattling fight for it; but Cooramen had the foot of him, and a turn better in point of condition. He answered the whip as if he hadn't gone a yard. I won cleverly, with a length to the good.

What a roar and storm of cheers there was all over the course! I didn't think it was so popular a win. But everybody knew he was George Barker's horse—a poor man's (comparatively) against a big squatter's. Jack Hall had a good many friends; and of course Possie had *her* share of well-wishers.

Possie rode up to the weighing yard with me, side by side, her eyes sparkling, and her face full of joy and triumph. Mr. Burdock had another case of champagne sent down to his buggy, and made everybody come and drink my health. He fell across Thoresby and his daughter, and would have no denial. They must come too.

'It's no use talking,' he said. 'I know every girl on the course is in love with my young friend at the present time. A good-looking young jock as has just won a big race, and rode it with judgment from end to end, is a man a young woman can't help admiring. So fill up, ladies and gentlemen, and here's Mr. Claythorpe's jolly good health, as is a rising man in the district, and will be heard of yet, take my word for it.'

Of course this was all very nice and pleasant, and as I stood there with the men drinking towards me, and the girls smiling and blushing and making believe to be angry with old Burdock, I could hardly believe I was Jesse Claythorpe at all. Not so long ago a farmer's boy, and in great doubt now and then where the next dinner was to come from. Wasn't this another world—a new world in every way?—a sort of heaven, only that we were not dead; where we had all kinds of pleasures and feelings and surroundings that we never dreamed of before!

Like most people when they're young, it seemed to me as if hardly anybody died. Poor mother was gone; but that was in England, and it seemed so long ago—so far off. My head began to feel dizzy with these thoughts, though of course I had never drank anything (I wasn't going to break my rule for anybody), and for that matter, nobody tried to make me. They never do in this country, once a man says 'no,' and means to stick to it. People talk about temptation, but they tempt themselves, it's my opinion.

Possie and Nellie Thoresby were standing next to Mr. Burdock, with an Honourable

Mr. Berkeley on the other side, who was talking nineteen to the dozen to Possie, and she laughing and chaffing away with him, as if she'd known lords and swells all her life. She looked her best that day, and certainly took the shine out of Nellie Thoresby, who was a quiet steady-going girl, though she had something to say for herself too. She was not so tall as Possie, but well set in figure, and with a nice good-humoured face, as if nothing could put her out of temper. Everybody liked her about there, and respected her, which was more. However, the quietest girls can be roused up a bit at times, I've noticed, especially when there's another woman in the way. So when, after a deal of chaff with Mr. Burdock, Mr. Berkeley said he'd back Miss Barker for all he was worth to take the highest leap on the course; when I heard Nellie Thoresby say she'd ride her horse Wallaroo over the steeple-chase jumps against any other horse ridden by a lady, the best of three trials to win, I wasn't so much astonished as I should have been the week before the races.

'That's the very thing I wanted,' said

Possie, 'you're the best girl I know, Nellie. I was dying for a little bit of real riding, and I know Wallaroo can jump like a flying buck.'

'I'm afraid it's a silly affair, Possie; but as I've said so, I won't draw back.'

We went down and saw Cooramen, who was comfortable in his box, and none the worse for his race.

'When I saw you all coming up the straight,' Possie said, 'I thought I should have fainted with excitement. I saw the dear old horse was well up, but I wasn't sure you could land him. Ah yes! You rode splendidly. Everybody says so.'

'And what did you say?' I said. 'It was to please you I rode the race at all, and now I've won it, I suppose I've kept my word.'

'I'll tell you some day how pleased I was, and what I thought, though I didn't say it. But not just yet.'

She looked at me in a curious sorrowful sort of way, I thought. Though I didn't take much notice of it at the time, I often thought of it afterwards.

'I wish you were not going to ride over those jumps,' I said. 'I call that sort of thing foolishness, and I'm always afraid of a girl getting hurt.'

'I should have been killed long enough ago,' she said, 'if riding and falls would do it. I have had plenty of them in my time.'

'You may have one too many, but I'll see your saddle's properly girthed, at any rate. Jack Hall is just saddling the mare.'

· · · · · ·

It certainly was a pretty sight to see the two girls ride up the course till they came to within about fifty yards from the first steeple-chase leap. Giráh was ready to jump out of her skin, and she sidled and danced, and reared and plunged as if she was never going to steady down to her work. And through it all Possie sat quiet and as firm as a rock, with her hands down, and just yielding a little every time the mare rose from the ground, as if it was the easiest thing in the world. Wallaroo, a fine, solid, but active-looking horse, with a grand shoulder and capital legs, came stepping along quietly, but to my mind, looking more of a workman over timber than the other.

Two of the race stewards were chosen to start them and act as judges. Possie drew the winning lot. They were easy started. As she touched her rein the mare dashed off and raced at her first jump. She didn't attempt to hold her, but just steadied her. She went at the jump at an awful pace, but rose two lengths from the fence and made a splendid fly over it, clearing it with a foot to spare. As she went over Possie threw up her whip hand, sitting square, without the slightest waver or tremble in her saddle. I never saw a finer piece of riding in my life, and so thought the couple of thousand people at the races, or they wouldn't have cheered and shouted and thrown up their hats like a mob of schoolboys. The mare went on at full speed till she came to the next jump, clearing that and the one after in the same splendid style.

Then came Nellie Thoresby. She rode quietly at the first leap, which her horse cleared as easily as a cat jumping a footstool. The jump was exactly four feet high, made perfectly stiff, with heavy split-gum timber; so that they were no child's play. However, the bay horse hopped over them all as comfortable as a circus pony, measuring his distance and not touching a rail.

The next round was like the first; neither horse touched or baulked. Possie's mare had the most showy style of jumping; but the bay horse took his leaps in an easy well-mannered sort of way, and Nellie appeared so much at home in the saddle that not a word could be said against either.

The judges then called them up and told them to go over the leaps side by side, and to ride pretty fast, like a real steeple-chase.

So they went off, but as they got close to the first fence, Giráh went away, and racing at it, went up in the air as if she was never coming down again. I never saw a finer jump; and there was Possie as quiet and composed, with her hands before her, as if she was riding along a road. Wallaroo was close beside her, and being roused up a bit, made a grand jump, every bit as good in its way.

As the girls went at the next leap together, both horses put on a spurt, and the pace they made was a caution. All of a sudden I saw Possie pull her mare to the off-side, and send her at the 'wing.' This was fully six inches higher than the other part of the leap, made so purposely, to edge the horses into the regular panels. Giráh went at it as if a foot was no matter one way or the other, and every one held their breath, when all of a sudden a dog ran out of the crowd just in front of her fore legs. Now the mare was an awfully timid animal. I'd seen her shy and plunge when a bird flew up. The dog startled her, and I saw her change her leg. At the pace she was going there was no stopping or pulling off. Whether it was that, or half looking at the brute as she rose—it came to the same thing. She took off too far from the leap, and hitting the top rail an awful clout, came down on her head, rolled over poor Possie, and making a half turn over again from the way she had on, lay as still as a log. Her neck was broken, and she never stirred again.

Nellie Thoresby took the leap lower

down, clear and well. Why couldn't poor rash Possie have done the same thing? Pulling her horse up short before she came to the next leap, she slipped off, let him go, and was round holding up poor Possie's head almost before any one else had got up to her. She was terribly crushed, and one arm was broken. She was not insensible, and as I lifted her up she tried to smile, and whispered: 'Poor Giráh; it's our last ride. All my own fault, too. Mind you win the Town Plate, Jesse. If I can sit up, I'll come to the window to see it.'

We carried her into the nearest hotel, where she was laid on a bed and attended to. There was a doctor at the meeting, of course, so everything was done for her that could be. He set her arm and collar bone; but said he was afraid of internal injuries.

I can't bear to think about it, even now all these years have past. It seems like yesterday, and I can see her pale face as we lifted her up, and the pitiful smile she gave when she saw me and Nellie Thoresby by her.

She died that night. Nothing could have

saved her, the doctor said. She was brought home and buried at Boree by the side of her mother. George Barker said she couldn't rest anywhere else, he knew. She'd always said she'd like to be buried there, down by the creek, and under a spreading wilga tree. She always had an idea she'd die young, too, and told me so more than once.

Mr. Burdock and I went back to Wallanbah next morning, and a lot of the people cleared out, though I suppose the races were run somehow or other. I found that Leighton had come back there, and a lot of men with him that had just been paid off a big fencing contract. They were steady fellows, and Leighton said he'd taken the pledge for five years, and intended to keep it this time.

I found a letter there waiting for me from Mr. Buffray, offering me the management of Yugildah. He said he could see now where the trouble had been between me and Roper. It was partly his own fault, he said, as he had been too careless and easy-going, though he had heard stories from time to time. He would give me two hundred a year to manage the place, with, of course, a house to live in, and everything paid. If I couldn't go there myself, I was to get a good stockman and put him on as working-overseer. I could keep an eye on him from Yantara, and see that the accounts, etc., were right. He had too much to do to come up himself. From what he heard, Roper was safe to be convicted, and serve him right, too.

I had a long talk with Mr. Burdock, the end of which was that I offered Jack Hall the place at £70 a year and his rations. Burdock said he was getting rid of the cattle, and wouldn't want a smart man like Hall, and he wouldn't stand in the way of his bettering himself. So I went over with Jack and put him in charge. He knew the run like a book, and I knew I could trust him. I agreed with Leighton and some of the best men of the lot to go back with me to Yantara.

I was sick and tired of doing nothing, and mad to get at hard work and hard living for a while to knock poor Possie's miserable end out of my head—or help to, anyway. Day and night she was before me for months and months afterwards. However, work must be done, so we drafted the sheep, and away we went. The weather was hot, but we were too tired and hard-worked, what with watching and one thing and another, to think whether it was hot or cold.

After a bit I left the sheep to come on, and took Leighton and a couple of men with me to put up huts and yards. By the time they came up we were ready for them, and all went on well. The season was good—plenty of grass and water, that makes everything go well—not like some seasons we've had since. As for Leighton, there couldn't be a better man. He was like lots of people in this country that I've met, high and low. He had only *one fault*. But he kept right this time, and he put me up to everything I didn't know about stock and station life, and helped me in other ways, as a man brought up like him could.

When we got to Yantara we all worked double tides, in a manner of speaking. The season helped us along. We had a grand lambing, and I bought some more sheep on bills before shearing, and did well out of them too.

. . . . . .

There's not much more to tell after this.

Everything I touched did well, and I was able in a couple of years to pay off my debt to Mr. Burdock. I got as much credit as I wanted on my own account. I kept breeding up at Yantara, and sold one of the blocks for more money afterwards than the whole thing cost me.

As soon as everything was fairly started I left Leighton to manage by himself, and came over to Yugildah to live. I made myself fairly comfortable; had a decent cottage, a garden and plenty of vegetables. No man need live like a blackfellow in the bush unless he wants to.

After about two years, though I hadn't got poor Possie clear out of my head, I thought it was no use living solitary all my life, so, as I used to go to Thoresby's a good deal, and Nellie, curious to say, hadn't married, I asked her one day if she thought she could live at Yugildah and help me keep house, for there had come to be a deal of visitors and neighbours that called there now. She asked me why I didn't make up to one of the Miss Burdocks. I said they were too grand for me altogether.

So she said she'd consider about it. And the end of it was we were married, and no man ever had a better wife.

If I prospered before, be sure I didn't go back when I had a sensible prudent wife, with as good a head as she had heart, and a little more colonial experience than I had.

I was as happy as the day was long. Yugildah paid well, and we didn't find it necessary to take other people's calves. Roper got three years' imprisonment when he was tried at the Quarter Sessions, and the Judge told him he had a great mind to give him five.

Yugildah was a pleasanter place than Yantara, so we made our home there, and I went over there every now and then to see how things got on. Leighton kept his word and never touched a drop after he took the pledge, which of course made a different man of him. He dressed well and respected himself, and as the manager of Yantara, and being always a gentleman, with first-rate manners when he liked, he was received at the squatters' houses on equal terms.

After this Mr. Buffray took it into his head

to sell Yugildah, and offered it to me on long credit. I saw my way to make it pay for itself in five years—and so it did.

Shortly after Nellie Thoresby and I were married, sister Jane came up to see us. She and Nellie made great friends, and she was astonished to see how much I'd done. 'You've been helped greatly, Jesse,' she says, 'and you've had wonderful good friends—few men better—but they wouldn't have been so true to you if you hadn't been *true to yourself*. It was a lucky day when we sailed away from old England, wasn't it?'

While we were there, who should come over but Mr. Leighton. He dressed well now, and except that he was tanned and weather-beaten, couldn't have looked more like a swell in England. He and Jane had such long talks about Applegate and the old home, until Nellie and I began to laugh at Jane about the way he was interested in her village histories. By George! it was no joke after all. They took a fancy to one another, and though he was double her age, he was a dashing fellow to look at, after all. And there's something in an old friend and a long pedigree, especially in a woman's eyes. Jane was a fresh English-looking young woman, with a good figure and a pleasant face. He hadn't been in the way of seeing girls like her for many a year, so that was the reason he was struck with her, I suppose. He told her plain enough how low he had fallen—had given himself up for lost—and that she must take the chance of his keeping his word. If he broke it, all would be lost; and, of course, I tried to persuade her all I knew, besides saying (as Burdock did) that only one hard drinker in a thousand ever was really reclaimed when they got to that stage.

However, woman-like, she took the risk and thought it would be a wonderful thing to save a soul, and so on. He turned out to be *the* one in a thousand, luckily for her, and never went back on his pledge to his dying day. Jane and he were married and went to live at Yantara, where they were snug enough, though it was a deal hotter than Bandra.

Well, as time went on, I did better and better. Money's like a snowball—it keeps getting bigger as it rolls. Mr. Buffray made up his mind to sell Bandra and live near Sydney (where he had a beautiful place) for the sake of the children's education.

I bought it—to make a long story short—and there my wife and I, and all you boys and girls have been living for years. Mr. Leighton and his wife and family are at Yugildah. He's saved money, and had some sent out from home besides lately, with which he bought a half share in Yantara, where there's fifty thousand sheep now. They intend to go to England next year, to see his people and travel for a year or two. They'll leave their two eldest sons at school, so they say.

But I'm not going home—not a yard. Bandra's quite good enough for me, and as long as I have good health, good children, good horses, with enough to keep me from idling, and the best wife in the world, my home's here in Australia.

MESSRS. MACMILLAN AND CO.'S PUBLICATIONS.

BY THE SAME AUTHOR.

ROBBERY UNDER ARMS.

A STORY OF LIFE AND ADVENTURE IN THE BUSH AND IN THE GOLD-FIELDS OF AUSTRALIA.

A New Edition. Crown 8vo. 3s. 6d.

GUARDIAN—"A singularly spirited and stirring tale of Australian life, chiefly in the remoter settlements. . . . Altogether it is a capital story, full of wild adventure and startling incidents, and told with a genuine simplicity and quiet appearance of truth, as if the writer were really drawing upon his memory rather than his imagination."

SPECTATOR—"We have nothing but praise for this story. Of adventure of the most stirring kind there is, as we have said, abundance. But there is more than this. The characters are drawn with great skill. Every one of the gang of bushrangers is strongly individualised. A book of no common literary force."

THE SQUATTER'S DREAM.

New Edition. Crown 8vo. 3s. 6d.

SATURDAY REVIEW—"It is not often that stories of colonial life are so interesting as Mr. Boldrewood's *Squatter's Dream*. There is enough story in the book to give connected interest to the various incidents, and these are all told with considerable spirit, and at times picturesqueness. There is hardly a phase of a colonial squatter's life some twenty years ago of which we do not get a glimpse in the course of this lively and pleasant little volume."

FIELD—"In the present volume there is no straining after effect, but the routine of squatting life, with its good and bad seasons, the habits of such of the natives as are met with, the speculations of financiers, and the dangers of explorers, are skilfully depicted."

THE MINER'S RIGHT.

A TALE OF THE AUSTRALIAN GOLD-FIELDS.

New Edition. Crown 8vo. 3s. 6d.

ATHENÆUM—"The picture is unquestionably interesting, thanks to the very detail and fidelity which tend to qualify its attractiveness for those who like excitement and incident before anything else."

SPEAKER—"There are many good things in it."

PALL MALL GAZETTE—"The three volumes are brimful of adventure, in which gold, gold-diggers, prospectors, claim-holders, take an active part."

A COLONIAL REFORMER.

New Edition. Crown 8vo. 3s. 6d.

GLASGOW HERALD—"One of the most interesting books about Australia we have ever read."

SATURDAY REVIEW—"Mr. Boldrewood can tell what he knows with great point and vigour, and there is no better reading than the adventurous parts of his books."

MACMILLAN AND CO., LONDON.

MESSRS. MACMILLAN AND CO.'S STANDARD NOVELS.

UNIFORM EDITION OF THE NOVELS OF
F. MARION CRAWFORD.

In Crown 8vo, Cloth extra, 3s. 6d. each.

MR. ISAACS: a Tale of Modern India. Portrait of Author.
DR. CLAUDIUS: A True Story.
A ROMAN SINGER.
ZOROASTER.

MARZIO'S CRUCIFIX.
A TALE OF A LONELY PARISH.
PAUL PATOFF.
WITH THE IMMORTALS.
GREIFENSTEIN.
SANT' ILARIO.

A CIGARETTE-MAKER'S ROMANCE.

UNIFORM EDITION OF
MRS. CRAIK'S WORKS.

(The Author of "John Halifax, Gentleman.")

In Crown 8vo, Cloth extra, 3s. 6d. each.

OLIVE. With Illustrations by G. BOWERS.
THE OGILVIES. With Illustrations by J. McL. RALSTON.
AGATHA'S HUSBAND. With Illustrations by WALTER CRANE.
HEAD OF THE FAMILY. With Illustrations by WALTER CRANE.
TWO MARRIAGES.
THE LAUREL BUSH.
MY MOTHER AND I. With Illustrations by J. McL. RALSTON.
MISS TOMMY: A Mediæval Romance. With Illustrations by FREDERICK NOEL PATON.
KING ARTHUR; Not a Love Story.
SERMONS OUT OF CHURCH.

RE-ISSUE OF THE SIXPENNY EDITION OF
CHARLES KINGSLEY'S NOVELS.

Medium 8vo, Sewed, Price 6d. each.

WESTWARD HO!
HYPATIA.
YEAST.
ALTON LOCKE.

TWO YEARS AGO.

HEREWARD THE WAKE.

MACMILLAN AND CO., LONDON.

www.ingramcontent.com/pod-product-compliance
Lightning Source LLC
Chambersburg PA
CBHW031737230426
43669CB00007B/375